Canada and Quebec, Past and Future:
An Essay

This is Volume 70 in the series of studies commissioned as part of the research program of the Royal Commission on the Economic Union and Development Prospects for Canada.

This volume reflects the views of its author and does not imply endorsement by the Chairman or Commissioners.

Canada and Quebec, Past and Future: An Essay

DANIEL LATOUCHE

Published by the University of Toronto Press in cooperation with the Royal Commission on the Economic Union and Development Prospects for Canada and the Canadian Government Publishing Centre, Supply and Services Canada

University of Toronto Press
Toronto   Buffalo   London

Grateful acknowledgment is made to the following for permission to reprint previously published and unpublished material: Alain Stanké; Boréal Express; Éditions de l'Homme; Éditons La Presse; Éditions Libre Expression; Leméac; McGraw-Hill Ryerson Ltd.; Methuen Publications; David P. Shugarman.

©Minister of Supply and Services Canada 1986

Printed in Canada
ISBN 0-8020-7318-2
ISSN 0829-2396
Cat. No. Z1-1983/1-41-70E

CANADIAN CATALOGUING IN PUBLICATION DATA

Latouche, Daniel, 1945 –
  Canada and Quebec, past and future

(*The Collected research studies / Royal Commission on the Economic Union and Development Prospects for Canada,*
ISSN 0829-2396 ; 70)
Includes bibliographical references.
ISBN 0-8020-7318-2

1. Canada — Constitutional history. 2. Federal-provincial relations — Quebec (Province). 3. Canada — English-French relations. 4. Quebec (Province) — Politics and government — 1960– 5. Canada — Politics and government — 1963– I. Royal Commission on the Economic Union and Development Prospects for Canada. II. Title. III. Series: The Collected research studies (Royal Commission on the Economic Union and Development Prospects for Canada) ; 70.

FC2925.9.C66L38 1985   971.4'04   C85-099610-4

PUBLISHING COORDINATION: Ampersand Communications Services Inc.
COVER DESIGN: Will Rueter
INTERIOR DESIGN: Brant Cowie/Artplus Limited

CONTENTS

FOREWORD

When the members of the Rowell-Sirois Commission began their collective task in 1937, very little was known about the evolution of the Canadian economy. What was known, moreover, had not been extensively analyzed by the slender cadre of social scientists of the day.

When we set out upon our task nearly 50 years later, we enjoyed a substantial advantage over our predecessors; we had a wealth of information. We inherited the work of scholars at universities across Canada and we had the benefit of the work of experts from private research institutes and publicly sponsored organizations such as the Ontario Economic Council and the Economic Council of Canada. Although there were still important gaps, our problem was not a shortage of information; it was to interrelate and integrate — to synthesize — the results of much of the information we already had.

The mandate of this Commission is unusually broad. It encompasses many of the fundamental policy issues expected to confront the people of Canada and their governments for the next several decades. The nature of the mandate also identified, in advance, the subject matter for much of the research and suggested the scope of enquiry and the need for vigorous efforts to interrelate and integrate the research disciplines. The resulting research program, therefore, is particularly noteworthy in three respects: along with original research studies, it includes survey papers which synthesize work already done in specialized fields; it avoids duplication of work which, in the judgment of the Canadian research community, has already been well done; and, considered as a whole, it is the most thorough examination of the Canadian economic, political and legal systems ever undertaken by an independent agency.

The Commission's research program was carried out under the joint direction of three prominent and highly respected Canadian scholars: Dr. Ivan Bernier (*Law and Constitutional Issues*), Dr. Alan Cairns (*Politics and Institutions of Government*) and Dr. David C. Smith (*Economics*).

Dr. Ivan Bernier is Dean of the Faculty of Law at Laval University. Dr. Alan Cairns is former Head of the Department of Political Science at the University of British Columbia and, prior to joining the Commission, was William Lyon Mackenzie King Visiting Professor of Canadian Studies at Harvard University. Dr. David C. Smith, former Head of the Department of Economics at Queen's University in Kingston, is now Principal of that University. When Dr. Smith assumed his new responsibilities at Queen's in September 1984, he was succeeded by Dr. Kenneth Norrie of the University of Alberta and John Sargent of the federal Department of Finance, who together acted as Co-directors of Research for the concluding phase of the Economics research program.

I am confident that the efforts of the Research Directors, research coordinators and authors whose work appears in this and other volumes, have provided the community of Canadian scholars and policy makers with a series of publications that will continue to be of value for many years to come. And I hope that the value of the research program to Canadian scholarship will be enhanced by the fact that Commission research is being made available to interested readers in both English and French.

I extend my personal thanks, and that of my fellow Commissioners, to the Research Directors and those immediately associated with them in the Commission's research program. I also want to thank the members of the many research advisory groups whose counsel contributed so substantially to this undertaking.

DONALD S. MACDONALD

At its most general level, the Royal Commission's research program has examined how the Canadian political economy can better adapt to change. As a basis of enquiry, this question reflects our belief that the future will always take us partly by surprise. Our political, legal and economic institutions should therefore be flexible enough to accommodate surprises and yet solid enough to ensure that they help us meet our future goals. This theme of an adaptive political economy led us to explore the interdependencies between political, legal and economic systems and drew our research efforts in an interdisciplinary direction.

The sheer magnitude of the research output (more than 280 separate studies in 70+ volumes) as well as its disciplinary and ideological diversity have, however, made complete integration impossible and, we have concluded, undesirable. The research output as a whole brings varying perspectives and methodologies to the study of common problems and we therefore urge readers to look beyond their particular field of interest and to explore topics across disciplines.

The three research areas, — *Law and Constitutional Issues*, under Ivan Bernier; *Politics and Institutions of Government*, under Alan Cairns; and *Economics*, under David C. Smith (co-directed with Kenneth Norrie and John Sargent for the concluding phase of the research program) — were further divided into 19 sections headed by research coordinators.

The area *Law and Constitutional Issues* has been organized into five major sections headed by the research coordinators identified below.

- Law, Society and the Economy — *Ivan Bernier and Andrée Lajoie*
- The International Legal Environment — *John J. Quinn*
- The Canadian Economic Union — *Mark Krasnick*

- Harmonization of Laws in Canada — *Ronald C.C. Cuming*
- Institutional and Constitutional Arrangements — *Clare F. Beckton and A. Wayne MacKay*

Since law in its numerous manifestations is the most fundamental means of implementing state policy, it was necessary to investigate how and when law could be mobilized most effectively to address the problems raised by the Commission's mandate. Adopting a broad perspective, researchers examined Canada's legal system from the standpoint of how law evolves as a result of social, economic and political changes and how, in turn, law brings about changes in our social, economic and political conduct.

Within *Politics and Institutions of Government*, research has been organized into seven major sections.

- Canada and the International Political Economy — *Denis Stairs and Gilbert Winham*
- State and Society in the Modern Era — *Keith Banting*
- Constitutionalism, Citizenship and Society — *Alan Cairns and Cynthia Williams*
- The Politics of Canadian Federalism — *Richard Simeon*
- Representative Institutions — *Peter Aucoin*
- The Politics of Economic Policy — *G. Bruce Doern*
- Industrial Policy — *André Blais*

This area examines a number of developments which have led Canadians to question their ability to govern themselves wisely and effectively. Many of these developments are not unique to Canada and a number of comparative studies canvass and assess how others have coped with similar problems. Within the context of the Canadian heritage of parliamentary government, federalism, a mixed economy, and a bilingual and multicultural society, the research also explores ways of rearranging the relationships of power and influence among institutions to restore and enhance the fundamental democratic principles of representativeness, responsiveness and accountability.

Economics research was organized into seven major sections.

- Macroeconomics — *John Sargent*
- Federalism and the Economic Union — *Kenneth Norrie*
- Industrial Structure — *Donald G. McFetridge*
- International Trade — *John Whalley*
- Income Distribution and Economic Security — *François Vaillancourt*
- Labour Markets and Labour Relations — *Craig Riddell*
- Economic Ideas and Social Issues — *David Laidler*

Economics research examines the allocation of Canada's human and other resources, the ways in which institutions and policies affect this allocation, and the distribution of the gains from their use. It also considers the nature of economic development, the forces that shape our regional and industrial structure, and our economic interdependence with other countries. The thrust of the research in economics is to increase our comprehension of what determines our economic potential and how instruments of economic policy may move us closer to our future goals.

One section from each of the three research areas — The Canadian Economic Union, The Politics of Canadian Federalism, and Federalism and the Economic Union — have been blended into one unified research effort. Consequently, the volumes on Federalism and the Economic Union as well as the volume on The North are the results of an inter-disciplinary research effort.

We owe a special debt to the research coordinators. Not only did they organize, assemble and analyze the many research studies and combine their major findings in overviews, but they also made substantial contributions to the Final Report. We wish to thank them for their performance, often under heavy pressure.

Unfortunately, space does not permit us to thank all members of the Commission staff individually. However, we are particularly grateful to the Chairman, The Hon. Donald S. Macdonald; the Commission's Executive Director, J. Gerald Godsoe; and the Director of Policy, Alan Nymark, all of whom were closely involved with the Research Program and played key roles in the contribution of Research to the Final Report. We wish to express our appreciation to the Commission's Administrative Advisor, Harry Stewart, for his guidance and advice, and to the Director of Publishing, Ed Matheson, who managed the research publication process. A special thanks to Jamie Benidickson, Policy Coordinator and Special Assistant to the Chairman, who played a valuable liaison role between Research and the Chairman and Commissioners. We are also grateful to our office administrator, Donna Stebbing, and to our secretarial staff, Monique Carpentier, Barbara Cowtan, Tina DeLuca, Françoise Guilbault and Marilyn Sheldon.

Finally, a well deserved thank you to our closest assistants: Jacques J.M. Shore, *Law and Constitutional Issues*; Cynthia Williams and her successor Karen Jackson, *Politics and Institutions of Government*; and I. Lilla Connidis, *Economics*. We appreciate not only their individual contribution to each research area, but also their cooperative contribution to the research program and the Commission.

IVAN BERNIER
ALAN CAIRNS
DAVID C. SMITH

The place of Quebec within the Canadian federation has, since the earliest days, been central to our political experience. Throughout our history, we have been compelled to rework the Confederation "bargain" between French and English, Quebec and Canada, in response to changing conditions and changing conceptions of the Canadian political community.

In the 1960s, social and economic changes in Quebec combined with the growth of government to generate a state-centred, secular nationalism which challenged the federal system in new ways. These developments culminated in the Parti Québécois government, elected November 1976, and in the subsequent battle between rival conceptions of Quebec and Canada, which were personified in René Lévesque and Pierre Trudeau. The 1980 referendum, the 1982 patriation of the Constitution, and the 1985 defeat of the Parti Québécois represented a victory for the federalist vision. Independentist nationalism appeared to be the victim not only of the political appeal of a federalism in which Quebec and Québécois could feel at home, but also of the declining faith in the efficacy of the state, on which modern nationalism placed such strong faith.

A generation of political conflict was replaced by an apparent calm in Quebec–Canada relations. But many questions remained unresolved. These not only included the immediate issue of whether it is possible to alter the terms of the 1982 settlement in order to secure Quebec's official approval of the *Constitution Act, 1982*, which was achieved over the bitter opposition of the Quebec government; they also include the longer-term question of relations between the two linguistic communities at a time of greater continental integration and rapid economic change. Whatever the constitutional forms, they must reflect a partnership that is consistent with the aspirations of both language groups. The issue is not so much a question of whether Canada must be based on some sense of equality between its two great linguistic communities but on how to define that equality and how to represent it in our political institutions.

These are the issues at the heart of this monograph. Daniel Latouche reconstructs the history of the past generation in order to speculate on the elements of future accommodation. His analysis of the past is a revisionist one. He stresses the continuity of the events of the 1960s with earlier periods. He finds in the Quiet Revolution and its aftermath not clarity but doubt, ambiguity, chance, and political expediency. Similarly, he finds inconsistency and doubt in the English-Canadian response. Having himself been a partisan in the events he describes, as an adviser in the Lévesque government, Latouche provides a unique perspective on the inability to reconcile competing visions.

We now face an economic, social, and international environment very different from that which fueled the developments of the 1960s. New conditions and new leaders force new definitions of the situation. Latouche explores the implications of these factors as he sets forth his ideas for the possibilities of accommodation in the future. His guiding theme is the mutual dependence of Quebec and Canada: what serves the development of Quebec society is good for all of Canada, and vice versa; it is necessary to think of the alternatives in terms other than a zero-sum game. The result is an engaging and stimulating essay in interpretation.

RICHARD SIMEON

ACKNOWLEDGMENTS

All the ideas that go to make up this study, all the interpretations and suggestions, good and not so good, feasible and unrealistic have been formed after long discussions, not always serious but always fascinating, with Daniel Drache, Michel Lacombe, Denis Blais, Christiane Théberge and Denise Courteau. Gérard Bergeron showed himself to be a model of patience; he has not only read and re-read the text, but has listened many times over to what must have seemed a real theatre of improvisation. François Desrocher revised the entire text. His comments and those of certain members of the research staff of the Commission were very valuable. I only hope that they will not be too disappointed upon reading the modifications that I made to their comments.

I modified in the same way numerous ideas and comments gathered during my years on the Canadian constitutional "circuit." Richard Simeon, John Meisel, Claude Morin, Claude Ryan and André Bernard played a major role here.

Those who are offended by the rather iconoclastic style have only the members of the Department of Political Science of the University of British Columbia to blame. They are the ones who forced a poor graduate student from Quebec to reflect on the issues of this study. Don Smiley, Alan Cairns, Ed Black and Jean Laponce are the main guilty ones.

Le Devoir has published a great deal of my literary efforts, which has allowed me to refine my ideas and expose them to the harsh reality of opinion. The role of this newspaper in establishing an intelligent debate cannot be underestimated. Without this paper it would have been impossible to react, to question and to start heated debates.

And finally, if this study seems like a testament, it is not by accident.

Canada, constitutional questions, Quebec-Canada relations, federal-provincial conflicts: all this is certainly very important, but the chance must be given to others to get involved. It is similar to boy-scouts: it is important to join. But it is more important to quit. There is nothing more temporary than a last will and testament!

This said, and all the normal precautions having been taken, let's go . . . once again!

DANIEL LATOUCHE

Before We Get Going . . .

Some time ago, Canada finished going through "the most significant crisis in its history." In fact, Canada is not going through anything any more. This pleases some, who take the opportunity to point out how this has become a "normal" country, with its own constitution, national anthem, and flag. At last! Others will prefer to recall nostalgically how wonderful it was in those years when everything was on the table in endless last-ditch conferences.

Canada's political crisis has indeed lost something of its acuteness. But what are we to infer from this lull — that the crisis has been completely dealt with, or that it never truly existed? Not that this matters. The fact remains that Canada is now equipped with a new constitution which it can alter as it pleases; that the country's bilingual character is now entrenched in the law and political practice of the land; that francophones are being called to leadership in politics and other areas; and that arrangements are in the process of being made to effect the entry of the aboriginal groups into the Canadian mosaic.

Little Flags and Real Problems

Let us dispose of one cliché right at the outset — the contention that these changes are artificial (changes always have an air of unreality) or that they have not dealt with the "real" problems, among them the problem of Quebec and its place in the Canadian federation. This approach, beyond displaying the political bias of its adherents, presupposes that there exists, somewhere in the deepest soul of the people of a nation, a definition of their national problem. Thus, there is talk of the

"French evil" and the "British disease." This worldwide distribution of national disorders would be worth a lengthy disgression in itself, particularly in terms of the role of the media in creating a global frame of reference. There is no Quebec problem, irreducible and resistant to any attempt to solve it, any more than there is a Quebec mystery or a Canadian syndrome.

This tradition of the enigma is solidly established in custom. A well-known book was entitled, *Le sphinx parle français*, presumably meaning that in the Canada of 1965, everything incomprehensible in the language of political power was necessarily expressed in French. This way of viewing everything as a problem and a mystery does have some advantages, however. It allows it to be said that, despite all defeats, Quebec's cause persists (a subtle revenge by the conquered, or at least by those who think of themselves as such). This is a good enough way of signalling that the whole process has to begin again. The persistence of the "mystery" view also allows the conquerors to absorb their triumph more readily. This is when we hear about an "unfinished agenda," as if Quebec were only one item on a list, and had not yet been tackled, because of time, and had been deferred to the next meeting. This approach, however, implies that not too much time should be wasted on this old agenda. There are so many real problems clamouring for our attention.

Certainly, when we look at the situation of the Canada of the 1980s, "the worst crisis in its history", (that of the 1960s) seems tame indeed. When we compare the Canadian performance with that of the other industrialized countries, the deterioration here is obvious. This goes for the standard of living, the share of world trade, scientific research, productivity, life expectancy, support for the arts, industrial reconstruction, and employment. In some cases, we can no longer even talk about performance. Every week there is a new report to remind us that this country has fallen far behind its partners in the West. Accustomed as we are to administrative guerrilla action, we have virtually stopped paying attention to these bulletins of misfortune, and the same goes for the endless praise of made-in-Canada successes: the space arm, Telidon, CANDU, the LRT train, and fibre optics.

What a contrast this is to the 1950s, when Canada seemed literally stuck in second place in everything, a little behind the United States and, at times, feeling the odd impertinent shove from Sweden, our eternal rival and the source of comparisons. Canada was never first, except of course in hockey, but it was never last either. Rare indeed in those days were excited announcements about Canadian achievements; and even rarer, with good reason, were the little Canadian flags. It was a time when this country was satisfied to be second in everything, silently. Nowadays, what a ruckus there would be if we were to announce so little achievement!

To save face, the points of comparison are now selected with care: Canada is doing more than France for university research; the crime rate is lower in Canada than in the United States; we spend more than Germany for oceanographic research. No longer are there all-round comparisons.

Merely attending to Canada's image is enough, and not just any image either; it is one of a distinct Canadian reality, comfortable in its symbols. The country has nothing to say any more, or to offer, but this is said and offered with a brio which Canada did not know it had and which has so far succeeded in obscuring the fact that its weight has been purely symbolic. Form and appearance have emerged as unremitting concerns. Rather than truly building the country, we simply identify all possible reasons for saying or writing the word *Canada*, as if this were a magic formula, a sort of Tibetan prayer wheel that we turn for pleasure and to persuade ourselves that we exist.

For example (and this is merely one small detail among thousands, which are all just as insignificant), a single sheet of official letterhead from the Royal Commission on the Economic Union and Development Prospects for Canada mentions the word *Canada* at least five times. There is also a Canadian flag and the country's coat of arms. All this is on the letterhead and does not include the five *Canadas* that appear on the envelope or the three in the address. A recent letter from Statistics Canada contained no fewer than three Canadian flags, in full colour, together with a promotional message about the "six and five" program and half a dozen *Canadas* strewn around the page. Obviously, these are mere details and it would be petty to dwell on them.

In strictly political terms, the Canadian performance is scarcely more dazzling, but nobody seems to be shocked: apparently, questions of this kind no longer interest anyone. The vacuum is astonishing, and this zero point in political expression bodes ill. A number of Western countries are currently involved in original experiments to get themselves out of the crisis and back into position on the world chessboard. In France, Britain, Sweden, Italy, and the United States the experiments are going on: voters will soon pass judgment on the quality of this experimentation. In Canada, on the other hand, even the latest electoral swing has left us unconvinced of its deep ideological meaning. As far as ideology goes, our parties seem to be interchangeable. Canadians ration their time between waiting for American interest rates to go down and worrying that they will go up again.

It is a little unjust, of course, to state the problem in these simplistic terms, but there is always injustice when it comes to problems. We are waiting for more in Canada than a mere drop in U.S. interest rates. We are also waiting for the next Liberal leader, the next cabinet, the next last-ditch conference or new-beginning conference, the next election . . . and so on.

A Voyage in Time

Meanwhile, voices drift up from the past expressing two distinct and one-sided positions. These issues were supposed to have been dealt with; one hoped they had been forgotten. In the winter of 1984, the Manitoba language question seemed to be trying to take the whole Canadian political stage, surfacing right in the middle of the Liberal party's leadership race — a curious meeting of past and future.

The Manitoba question is more significant than it appears at first glance. Some see it as confirming their thesis, while others conclude from it that the triumph of a particular vision of Canada has not yet been attained. These reactions are as spontaneous as they are predictable. Even the Franco-Manitobans seem to have decided to make this another special moment in their tragic story.

Quite apart from what this Manitoba debate reveals about the prejudices still held by a good number of Canadians, it is sad and distressing because it pushes us a long way backwards, such a long way that we have to ask ourselves whether the period 1960–80 was really as important as people like to think, especially those who played a part in it. One might have expected, with the *Official Languages Act*, the new *Canadian Charter of Rights and Freedoms*, the agreements of the three large federal parties and all the opinion leaders in the Quebec government and the various provincial governments, plus the toughness of Manitoba's NDP government (in short, with everything Canada has of good sense and vision) that this issue would have been resolved in terms of the most elementary justice. All the compromises had been worked out, with practical constraints being taken into account and provision made for a flexible schedule and periodic evaluations. Yet nothing came of it all. Worse still, the question was not even dealt with one way or the other. It died on the House order paper, an inglorious fate if ever there was one. We now have to wait for the judges to decide. More waiting.

So swift an appeal to judicial interpretation tells us something of the bankruptcy of the compromise worked out at recent constitutional conferences. The meetings had no reason for taking place except to rehabilitate the political process and to let Canadians take charge of developing the collective contract that unites them. Despite the fact that all preliminary conditions had been met — political and constitutional, as well as administrative and judicial — the Manitoba language issue could not be resolved by the normal workings of institutions and political power. Once again, Manitoba has reminded us that our real country is very different from the one built and rebuilt by the elites at their conferences. This is not the first time Manitoba has played this role. It played it in the last century too. We could almost talk about a mission.

It is against the wall of this real country, so rarely consulted, that the best-laid plans come to grief. This fresh setback has exposed the weakness of our political-administrative structures and has shown what little substance they have in the face of reality. My point here is not to take a position against elites that are supposedly enlightened but are too far ahead of a population which has finally been able to give its prejudices full rein. That would be too simple. Besides, the arguments heard in this affair from the Manitoba Conservative party, a full member of the right-thinking community, show us how weak the progressive bloc really is.

Rather, what we need to retain from the Manitoba episode is that the very idea of a "vision of the country", about which so much has been written, finds virtually no echo in the Canadian people. A strong majority of Manitobans rejected not so much the rights of francophones or the place of the French language, but the very idea that a collectivity could and should, through a government decision and through action by the state, mobilize to give direction to its future development. The Manitoba story illustrates a refusal to work from models, no matter how liberal they are or how they conform to reality.

People are refusing to take positions on their history and their development, as if these things were beyond anyone's reach and occurred only in terms of interaction among citizens. The refusal to intervene was clearly demonstrated in Manitoba, but it is by no means the exclusive property of that province. One of the central themes of this essay is that such refusal characterizes all of Canada and finds vigorous expression every time it gets a chance.

We should be greatly concerned by the fact that the Manitoba episode has already become part of Canadian political practice and mythology. No Canadians seem to have changed their minds in the wake of these events. They all saw what they wanted to see, as if nothing had actually happened.

In fact, perhaps nothing did happen. In the short term and even in the long term, perhaps nothing is going to change. The francophone community will continue to exist. Existing in such a context, however, necessarily means progressing and declining at the same time, like any minority community whose fate is important to the government. Nonetheless, we must ask ourselves what use the *Constitution Act* and the *Canadian Charter of Rights and Freedoms* are if their combined existence was unsuccessful in stopping the slippage and decline to which these francophone groups have fallen victim, and we should ask whether this failure does not also threaten the very survival of these groups. Strange indeed is Canada's political math: the logic of contradictions seems to operate by special rules.

Uncertain Mandate for an Uncertain Country

The Manitoba story leads me to note yet once more that this country's plans for political reconstruction have small chance of success. The rarefied atmosphere of the Canadian reality seems unsuitable for them. Is it even worth trying to achieve them?

For the Royal Commission on the Economic Union and Development Prospects for Canada, this is a worrisome question, or at least it ought to be. The very words chosen to identify the Commission speak of the general looseness in current thinking. The terms could have been transposed without changing their meaning:

- Royal Commission on Development of the Prospects for the Canadian Economic Union,
- Royal Commission on the Canadian Union and Development of Economic Prospects,
- Royal Commission on Development of the Canadian Union and its Economic Prospects.

What a contrast this is with the Royal Commission on Bilingualism and Biculturalism, whose very name defined a specific mandate — even too specific, since the commission was unable to carry it out.

At the risk of seeing more Manitoba-style outcomes, it is essential that we should conduct a thorough review of the way Canadian political practice and debate function. This is never easy, and certainly far less easy than handing out blame. As Manitoba's case shows so well, there is no urgency about this. The problem the Commission is looking at is so boundless that it is hard to give it a name. The Commission will be strongly tempted to invent emergencies in order to justify its mandate and the radical solutions which its organizational process presses it to suggest. After all, has one ever known a royal commission to decide that the situation was not urgent, that the challenges were not exciting, and that the solutions were not imperative? The proliferation of the Canadian media will surely facilitate the commissioners' work. We have a long-established habit, in fact, of peering into the smallest cavities in our collective experience in order to find ever more threatening dangers, especially if they concern Canadian unity, and to find challenges that are ever more intoxicating. Yesterday it was the "just society". Today it is the technological revolution.

The poverty of such diagnoses is not particularly worrisome in itself. It is part of the organizational culture of all commissions of inquiry. It is a rite that we gladly accommodate. The danger does not lie here; and should we even speak of danger when it is more an "anticipated disappointment"? The danger, or disappointment, arises from the fact that commissions often say more about a society's past, present, and future problems than about the solutions which could be put into effect.

We should here note the distinction between being part of the problem and being part of the solution. At present, all indications are that the Royal Commission on the Economic Union and Development Prospects for Canada is following the tradition of previous commissions of inquiry, which is to preserve for future generations the problems and solutions of the past. The fact that, this time, everything is clothed in references to the technological revolution, the realignment of the wheels of the world economy, and the need not to miss the main direction of the coming century, alters nothing. The ends of centuries, and especially the ends of millennia, always produce such an effect.

How will the Commission be able to meet the challenge of understanding that its mandate, its composition, and its intrinsic problems make it, too, a part of the Canadian problem? Nothing leads me to believe that it will be able to meet this challenge, but there is nothing really to prevent it doing so either.

This Commission is in the fortunate position that no one expects much from its labours, certainly not the new Conservative government. It may be, then, that it will surprise everyone by the originality of its arguments and by the accuracy of its analysis. To do this, it clearly will have to surprise itself a little. In this regard, it has to be said that the interim report presented by the commissioners leaves us very little hope. Rarely has one seen a document so lacking in intellectual breadth and originality. It exudes tedium and drudgery. All the clichés and facile images are mustered there in questions which pretend to give the picture of a highly complex situation. The commissioners have thought best to offer us their own version of Trivial Pursuit.

Speaking of a Difficult Mandate

The above remarks indicate more effectively than any warning that this present study is to be seen as an essay. It is, then, a personal reading of events. This was not the only possible approach. It is never easy to work without the safety net of scientific objectivity; not easy, but more exciting just the same. In Quebec's case, scientific essays and objective analyses are not lacking. An entire generation dedicated itself to this task with an energy that was constantly renewed. For 15 years, a number of us went to all the colloquies and all the conferences. With a good-natured lack of modesty, we made spectacles of ourselves in front of English-Canadians who were full of helplessness and good will. There is nothing, absolutely nothing, that we did not tell one another and then tell again. Today, this much-played record is worn out. All that remains is to find an elegant way of withdrawing it from circulation. This could be called a constitutional fade-out.

For someone such as myself, whose opinions on the future of Canada are well known, this was the only way to work. It is not every day, in fact, that a separatist contributes in this way to the work of a federal body. I must say that except for this Commission and a few bodies that are concerned about their scientific autonomy, such as the Social Sciences Research Council, any Québécois who is not prepared to accept the

"Canada equals federalism" equation is usually treated with the utmost contempt.

Is it still necessary to offer a warning to the readers of this essay? They will already have guessed that they will be confronted with an obvious mixture of journalism, speculation, savage judgment, and hypothesis. The words *always* and *never* abound in this text. By contrast, nuance is fairly rare. Corners are often turned smartly, and many paragraphs merit clarification. Quotations and footnotes are rare, except in one chapter where it was essential to let others speak. Obviously, a study without notes at the bottom of the page cannot be as objective as another!

I would like to make an apology to those whose thoughts have been distorted or simply ignored. It was inevitable, but perhaps inexcusable.

PART I

Retrospective on Canada-Quebec Relations

Chapter 1

The Real Starting Point of a Phony Debate

The story of the most recent phase of constitutional review begins during 1956 and not in June 1960 or in 1968 as we are taught by the official line. Like all important stories, ours opens innocuously, without fanfare, as if nothing was going on. Now that we know the sequel and, above all, the outcome of the whole episode, it is easier to search through its humble origins for the signs pointing to later developments. This is the aim of this first chapter.

Beware the Quiet Revolution

I shall be assigning much importance to the period before 1960, which is normally passed over in silence. It is so much easier, in fact, to use the arrival of Jean Lesage or Pierre Elliott Trudeau to mark the beginning of the modern era in Canada-Quebec relations. Clearly, having it all start up in 1960 involves arguing the intentional and not merely accidental nature of the challenge to these relations, as well as the role of catalyst which Quebec is supposed to have played. Thus, the mythic status of 1960 and the Quiet Revolution is once more confirmed. Quebec is made the leading actor of the piece, with Canada being the consenting partner. Moreover the expression, "Quebec-Canada," which we use so freely, has a certain unreality about it. It speaks of a view which finds no echo outside Quebec itself. But in a country that makes room for a *Quiet* Revolution and a *Progressive* Conservative party, this incongruity of language need surprise no one.

Nor should we be amazed to find that, later on, this dating leads irrevocably to the development of an official history of Quebec-Canada relations which rests on five statements:

1. Before 1960, Quebec, a traditional society par excellence, does not question its relations with the rest of Canada, being satisfied to practise a negative nationalism, shut in on itself. Taking advantage of this situation, Maurice Duplessis can turn the struggle against federal centralism to his own uses. This strategy allows him to maintain his electoral base while keeping Quebec in its traditional strait jacket.
2. With the Quiet Revolution, an unprecedented process of social change sweeps through Quebec. From being negative, French-Canadian nationalism becomes Québécois and positive. The business of catching up and achieving growth replace the mere defence of the province's treasurers. Quebec becomes a modern society.
3. Once entrenched in the provincial state, this nationalism rapidly brings into question the financial and judicial limitations imposed by federalism on the growth of the new national state. Confrontation with the central government and with English Canada is thus found right at the heart of the action plan of the Quiet Revolution.
4. Following repeated demands from Quebec for a new political status within the Canadian federation, all Canadian governments, federal and provincial, embark on a review of the constitutional framework to try to respond to the legitimate demands of the French province and, in so doing, adapt the *Constitution Act, 1867* to the new realities.
5. For all kinds of reasons (lack of understanding by English Canada, tactical errors, Ottawa's bad faith), the negotiations do not result in a new status for Quebec. There are many constitutional changes but no genuine reforms.

Each one of these statements could appropriately be developed, given the broad differences in interpretation that exist. On the whole, however, this chronology has become official. It can be divided into five major stages:

1. Quebec is waiting.
2. Quebec changes.
3. Quebec demands.
4. Canada listens.
5. Canada refuses.

With the chronology thus structured, the following stage must necessarily emerge from a very limited range of possibilities:

6a. Quebec renews its demands.
6b. Quebec gives up.
6c. Quebec falls asleep.
6d. Quebec dies.

This way of imagining the story of political relations between Quebec and Canada in fact simply moves the paradigm of the Quiet Revolution into this area. It is against the perspective of the Quiet Revolution that we now assess everything that has happened in Quebec during and after that very special period: economic development, social change, cultural transformation, and also constitutional negotiation. In short, the Quiet Revolution is supposed to have forced Quebec to reconsider the place it occupied within Canada.

We are far from unanimous, of course, in identifying the social forces which launched this catching-up process, and in saying who has profited most from it. Is it the nation, the middle class, the bureaucratic elite, or one of the many factions of the new petite bourgeoisie? There is agreement, however, on seeing the Quiet Revolution as a sufficient and necessary condition for the emergence of the constitutional dispute.

Thus, associating the birth of the Quebec-Canada debate with the Quiet Revolution — that mythic and very special period in the recent history of Quebec — can only result in posthumous glorification of the debate. One then drifts inevitably into political anthropomorphism, with statements like "For twenty years Quebec has been demanding . . . " (from which this present analysis is not exempt). This partly explains why, in 1984, Quebec's constitutional defeat was so readily seen as a cataclysm, at least by those who are perceived as the protagonists of the Quiet Revolution. The failure of the one was taken automatically as the anticipated failure of the other. Here is a relationship which it is high time to question. In fact, the constitutional debate has taken up only a very limited space in the accelerated change experienced by Quebec since 1960. At least, this is what I shall attempt to prove.

A number of researchers have already undertaken to put the Quiet Revolution in perspective, analyzing its real antecedents (Roy, 1976), its form (Latouche, 1974), and its scope (Gingras and Nevitt, 1983). The same analysis is called for in the constitutional area.

Openly attacking so rooted a paradigm is a dangerous business. For the past twenty years, all the research, including so-called critical work (Brunelle, 1978), has done nothing but confirm this perception. We must therefore be prepared to remove the facts from their context, to insist on some details, and to exaggerate certain interpretations a little. Like all paradigms, that of the Quiet Revolution has ended by prescribing its own formulas concerning the questions to ask, the areas to investigate and the answers to foresee. For many groups in Quebec society, this paradigm of the Quiet Revolution has become an important factor in the consolidation of their power. As such, it is reminiscent of paradigms which, in other societies and at other times, have played an identical role: the October Revolution in the U.S.S.R., the Resistance in France, the New Deal in the United States.

Soon, whether one has or has not been part of the Quiet Revolution will replace that other existential question — whether one did or did not experience the Depression. For the moment, however, it is preferable not to laugh at these things. Nonetheless, that is what I am going to do.

A scenario of the future based on such a paradigm would not be totally wrong. In any case, no scenario is ever quite that wrong. Our understanding of the options, however, might end up by looking like all those prognostications of a little while ago, hurriedly relegated to the waste-basket, which saw the future of Canada and Quebec in terms of "last chance," "final date," "inexorable movement," and "inevitable destiny." Today, we need another type of scenario, which bases itself on a real past, not on our vision of what might have been.

I make no claim to the rewriting of history. Besides, what could I rewrite? It surely cannot be denied that a clamour of voices from Quebec demanded a redefinition of Quebec's place in Canadian Confederation; or that the constitutional conference of 1981, along with the referendum of 1980, actually took place; and that these events marked significant advances in the story of Quebec-Canada relations. I am not challenging the events themselves so much as the rather grandiose meanings which are perennially read into them. A touch of humility will do our glorious constitutional history no harm.

My objective is to present two scenarios for the future of Quebec and its relations with Canadian society. The idea here is not simply to extrapolate from the official interpretation of the 1960–82 period. Such an exercise would be of limited value. At most, it would teach us a little more about the official version of this immediate past.

In order to escape the stranglehold of the Quiet Revolution a little, I have chosen to go back farther into the past. Our story thus does not begin in 1960 but in the preceding years; it was in those years that the stakes were named which would become the basis of the federal-provincial dispute, and it was then that the political and partisan strategies emerged which were to have such significance later on. In fact, one of my hypotheses is that it is the years from 1957 to 1963, roughly the John Diefenbaker interlude — and not the Quiet Revolution — which are decisive for our understanding of the development of the constitutional issue and Quebec-Canada relations.

So, "Once more, from the beginning," as the policeman said to the suspect.

The Beginnings of a Long, Long Story

It was in 1960 that the Liberal party of Quebec decided, for the first time, to incorporate proposals for change in the working of Canadian federalism into its official election platform. At that time, it must be said, the Liberal party had virtually gone out of business as far as federal-provincial matters were concerned.

In the election of 1956, the party had been skilfully outflanked by the Union Nationale and had been forced into a posture that was ambiguous to say the least. The Liberal leader, Georges-Émile Lapalme, had made a commitment to abolish double taxation and thus to forgo one of Quebec's main assets in the field of fiscal autonomy. Placed on the defensive, the party thereafter had to fall back on a position which had served it very badly in the previous election: accusing the Union Nationale of negativism.

> Provincial autonomy, far from being summed up in a *no*, requires a positive and constructive attitude on Quebec's part in supplying appropriate solutions for the problems in federal-provincial relations that have been created by the economic and social development of Canada (Roy, 1971, p. 367; translation).

This gave the Union Nationale a fine chance to make fun of the Liberal party's pirouettes. Never since the provincial tax was brought in had the provincial Liberals managed to reach a coherent position on it — this despite the fact that the *fait-accompli* quality of Maurice Duplessis' manoeuvre should have made their job easy for them. The Liberal party had also hoped to make hay out of the government's decision to lease the Ungava Territory to the Iron Ore Company. In the midst of the election campaign, however, here was the federal prime minister rushing to "congratulate the province on having reached this agreement" (*La Presse*, May 28, 1956; translation). Then, just when the Liberals were accusing the government of taxing Québécois excessively, and when they were challenging it to demonstrate the profitability of its nihilistic approach to federal-provincial relations, here was the federal government granting Quebec the right to go after an even bigger slice of the fiscal pie than the Liberal party itself wanted to get. It was ludicrous.

The provincial election of June 20, 1956 was a rout: Lapalme's group captured only 44.5 percent of the vote and a block of 20 seats. Some months later, the 1957 federal election exposed the weakness of the federal Liberal party. Then in 1958 John Diefenbaker had his stunning victory. The cooperation of the Union Nationale was not unrelated to Diefenbaker's surprising success in Quebec, even though we must not overestimate the effect this had; nor, above all, should we underestimate the attraction, not so much of Diefenbaker himself but of his will to give new impetus to Canada.

Diefenbaker's new Conservative team was hardly in tune with the people of Quebec, who had always returned the favour. Suddenly, the Conservative party was faced with an artificially inflated Quebec wing. For the first time since 1939, Quebec City and Ottawa would be run by political allies, and as in 1939, the federal partner was the one with the wind in its sails (LaTerreur, 1973, p. 174).

This spasm of election activity, federal as well as provincial, forced, among other things, a reexamination of the members of the two Liberal leadership teams, in a minuet that was typified more by chance than by orchestration.

In the spring of 1958, the Liberal party of Quebec held a leadership convention. This convention was supposed simply to confirm the position of Georges-Émile Lapalme, who was expected to have no serious opponents. Well, two challengers showed up, Paul Gérin-Lajoie and Jean Lesage. There were many things separating the three men, but they had this in common: they represented, each in his own way, the party's most anti-nationalist element. At the last moment, Lapalme withdrew.

Jean Lesage had been elected as the Liberal member for Montmagny-L'Islet in the federal election of 1945. With the conscription crisis in full swing at the time, he had distinguished himself by an all-out defence of Mackenzie King's referendum. After that, he had busied himself with economic matters (banks, pensions) and had never missed the chance to join a parliamentary delegation travelling abroad. In 1953, he had become minister of northern affairs and natural resources: he was one of the most ardent supporters of federal intervention in areas of provincial power. During a career of 13 years in Ottawa, he had never spoken up on behalf of francophone rights or the place of French-Canadians in the federal administration (Daignault, 1981).

Paul Gérin-Lajoie, Lesage's opponent at the leadership convention, had become known particularly for a highly technical study, published in English only, on the question of constitutional amendment in Canada. Defeated in a 1956 by-election, Gérin-Lajoie had done everything in his power to shed his intellectual image. He restricted his campaigning to topics of social reform, including education.

At the leadership convention, the themes of federal-provincial relations, of Quebec's place in Confederation, and of the language rights of French minorities outside Quebec went unraised by any of the candidates. And with good reason!

The Liberal posture of benign neglect on all these questions was confirmed when Duplessis died in 1959 and Paul Sauvé became leader of the Union Nationale. In resolving (or so it was believed at the time) the prickly issue of federal grants to universities, Sauvé deprived the Liberals of another hobby-horse and showed in practical terms that the slogan "Blue in Ottawa, blue in Quebec City" could indeed succeed the old "Blue in Quebec, red in Ottawa." With the death of Duplessis and Sauvé's famous "Henceforth. . . ," some political commentators ventured to forecast the end of the everlasting federal-provincial quarrels, and possibly even the demise of French-Canadian nationalism.

The case of federal grants to universities also tells us much about the dense political confusion which then obscured the federal-provincial field, as well as the difficulty that political parties had in translating these matters into straightforward partisan terms. From 1953 to 1959, Ottawa deposited money, designed for Quebec universities, into a fund which was supervised by the Canadian universities federation. These sums quickly rose to $25 million; but the Quebec government forbade the universities to share them, under threat of retaliation. As a substitute, the Quebec government paid the universities the equivalent of the federal grant every year, over and above the grants provided for by law. There never was, in the strict sense of the word, an attempt by Duplessis to starve the universities (Godin, 1980, vol. 2, p. 128).

For purely political reasons, the Diefenbaker government wanted to reach a rapid accommodation with the Sauvé government, which was perceived as being more flexible than its predecessor. Accordingly, a compromise was proposed: Quebec would be given one more point of corporate income tax if it agreed to pay its universities a sum equivalent to the federal grant. Noting that this agreement would merely make the federal intervention official, Paul Sauvé went back on his initial acceptance, and in December 1959 Ottawa-Quebec negotiations were in deadlock.

In the end, it was Premier Antonio Barrette who broke the log jam (Barrette, 1966). He invented a clever device which allowed all those involved to save face. To balance the fact that the federal portion was greater than the amount Ottawa intended to pay the Quebec universities, Quebec agreed to raise its own contribution to the per capita financing of its universities. This meant that Ottawa would not have to cut equalization payments to the province by as much. For all the oblivion into which it has fallen today, this episode proved crucial to the later federal-provincial dispute.

Already we can begin to sort out certain often-reiterated certainties about this period. The formula for fiscal compensation no more dates from the 1960s than the federal-provincial conflicts do. As regards Sauvé's talents as negotiator and conciliator, some modification is indicated here as well. The time probably has not yet come, however, to adjust the positive image of Paul Sauvé and his legend.

Still, this episode created the twofold Canadian tradition of opting out and of fiscal compensation in return for a change in constitutional arrangements. From that moment on, it became clear that political leaders could easily sidestep a double necessity: to respect the Constitution so that the country could be properly administered, and to work to change the Constitution in order to deal with problems which had not been foreseen in 1867.

It was against this background that Quebec prepared to turn the corner of the Quiet Revolution.

Making the Turn Unawares

In the fall of 1959, the Liberal party of Quebec was worried about its prospects. The choice of a new leader and the death of Duplessis did not seem to have brought it any closer to power. The Groupe de recherches sociales (GRS; Social Research Group) was asked to make the first public-opinion survey ever carried out for a Quebec political party. Its results had the effect of a cold shower on the electoral hopes of a party which, in addition, was no more successful at recruiting candidates than it was at developing an original political platform or an adequate financial base. The fact that the federal Liberal party was itself in opposition, and was led by a man who was more familiar with Egyptian internal politics than with those of Quebec, did not help much either.

The survey alone should necessitate a reexamination of all myths about the inevitability of the Quiet Revolution (GRS, 1960). The majority of voters said that they were unable to distinguish between the two parties except when it came to defence of provincial autonomy, on which the Union Nationale emerged as the clear winner. In addition, people thought that the Union Nationale's program, its team of representatives, and its leadership were superior. On the whole, they were relatively happy with the way things were going. One thing should be noted: the generation gap was not a discriminatory factor in party support, the young voters generally being carbon copies of their elders and sometimes even turning out to be a little more conservative. Urban-rural distinctions came out the most clearly. The least one can say is that the results of the 1960 election did not represent a backlash based on age group and youth.

Although it was much more clear-cut than the 1956 version, the Liberal election platform of 1960 still gave only limited emphasis to the federal-provincial field. Four of its clauses called for new official bodies, a move that is never very controversial. These were a department of interprovincial affairs, an interprovincial conference, an interprovincial secretariat, and an interprovincial council and constitutional tribunal. A single suggestion for constitutional change was put forward: repatriation of the *Constitution Act, 1867*. This particular clause (which was forgotten by the platform's main author, Georges-Émile Lapalme) was added at the eleventh hour by Paul Gérin-Lajoie and clearly reflected one of his favourite themes. The issue of Quebec-Canada relations was completely absent from this entire campaign.

Armed with the results of their 1959 survey, the Liberals decided on sweeping changes in their election strategy. They would not repeat the blunder of 1956, especially since Antonio Barrette's recent success on the universities question hardly left him open to attack on the grounds of respect for provincial jurisdiction or sterile nationalism. In their indecision, they chose simply not to refer to these things, a choice made easier for them by the fact that the party had nothing to say. Their strategy centred on a four-point approach (Hamelin and Gagnon, 1969; Lemieux, 1969):

- Never stop attacking in order to undermine the government team's credibility.
- Run a campaign at the local level and, in organizing it, copy the proven methods of the Union Nationale.

- At most, make a few autonomist noises, but without campaigning against Ottawa, in view of the unequivocal mandate which Quebec voters have just given the Conservative party.
- Stress the theme of aging and the need to give another team a chance.

During an interview given in 1974, Jean Lesage confirmed what was already an open secret: "Had Mr. Sauvé not died and had an election been held in June, I do not think we could have taken power. I would certainly have increased the number of Liberal members" (Cardinal, 1978, p. 46; translation).

In spite of a lustreless performance by the new premier, in spite of the scandals, in spite of support for the Liberals from broad sections of the media as well as from all intellectuals, and in spite of their professionally run campaign (compared with the improvisation that ran riot in the Union Nationale camp), the Liberal victory of 1960 was only won by a hair. It was going to take a strong dose of post facto historical reconstruction to make it into the tsunami of a new era. In Montreal, René Lévesque got in by 129 votes and Paul Gérin-Lajoie by 149. It was the hardest-fought contest in the political history of Quebec: 34 percent of members won with majorities slimmer than 5 percent. As tidal waves and hurricanes go, one had seen better. How fortunate that there should be the legend to give all this a little grandeur when it began with barely any.

At no point in the campaign was mention made of a necessary re-evaluation of Quebec-Canada relations. Compared with previous elections, the themes of respect for provincial autonomy, centralization and the battle to protect Quebec's treasures were practically nonexistent. In a fight pitting Jean Lesage against Antonio Barrette, such themes would have lacked credibility.

Obviously, this analysis does not tally with the widespread image of a downtrodden, pent-in Quebec, awaiting its destiny and a Quiet Revolution that would fling the doors of progress wide open. If such really was the situation, very few voters seem to have been aware of it. If a minority of them did switch allegiance at the last minute, they did so not so much as a result of generally adverse judgments on 16 years of Union Nationale administration, but in order to give a chance to another team — a team whose captain, moreover, seemed closer to the tradition of strong leaders (Duplessis, Sauvé) than his Union Nationale opponent did. The concept of political democracy as a seesaw between politicians whose differences are dimly perceived, and who in any case are not expected to do very much, has been well described by Pierre Trudeau (Trudeau, 1956, 1967).

Much later, when the Quiet Revolution's first mythic exegeses began to appear, a great deal would be made of a so-called catching-up of Quebec's political development in relation to an economic and social development which had already changed the profile of Quebec society considerably. We may ask ourselves, however, if any such political maturation was implied in the socioeconomic data.

The GRS survey, which was cited above, portrayed a population which had little interest in politics, which was not trying to be informed, and which was all but unaware of the political scandals involving members of the Union Nationale government. What counted for them was a good leader rather than well-made laws. In his study of the early days of public-affairs television on Radio-Canada, Gérard Laurence (1982, p. 228) clearly showed the limitations of public debate as it took place over the airwaves of the state corporation, which was nonetheless seen as a special launching ground for the Quiet Revolution. The issue of provincial politics took second place on these programs, the mere mention of whose names still brings pangs of nostalgia: "Carrefour," "Les idées en marche," "Conférence de presse," and "Point de mire", ("Crossroads," "Ideas on the Move," "Press Conference," and "Target"). Once again, we have to climb down: the Quiet Revolution was not a product of television. From a list drawn up in 1958, here are a few taboo topics that were better not dealt with on the air unless one wanted to see Parliament get a little too interested in Radio-Canada:

- certain delicate subjects that brought in a party's policy;
- most problems of provincial politics;
- strikes in progress;
- certain international conflicts involving friendly countries;
- any issue implicating a federal or provincial service; and
- any subject liable to be offensive to public opinion.

Thus, one should not exaggerate the importance of these public forums in preparing the events of 1960, and this is even more the case with the mass-audience programs. This was certainly not the time of conferences and colloquies on Quebec's place in "the Confederation of tomorrow." No specific demands were being made of the political system, whose shape was hard to discern. Here was a political culture in which nothing was insisted on, especially not constitutional change, but in which much was hoped for (Lemieux and Hudon, 1975; Heintzman, 1983).

The Federal-Provincial Conference of July 1960

In July 1960, a few weeks after taking office, Quebec's new Liberal government took part in the annual federal-provincial meeting. There, it voiced certain proposals that had been worked out, not on the basis of the recent election platform but in line with approaches used traditionally at these meetings. Other participants expressed no surprise at these suggestions, and the media focussed mainly on the bearing and self-assurance of Quebec's new premier. His proposals were as follows:

- the immediate resumption of talks on repatriation and the amending formula in order to erase the vestige of colonialism represented by the obligation to resort to the British Parliament to alter the Canadian Constitution;
- the inclusion in the repatriated Constitution of a charter of basic rights to guarantee the language and educational rights of the French-speaking minorities outside Quebec;
- the creation of a constitutional tribunal that would be distinct from the Supreme Court, since the latter could hardly be capable of objectivity when all its judges were appointed by the central government;
- the creation of a permanent federal-provincial secretariat;
- the convening of an annual meeting of provincial premiers so that the provinces could bring their positions into line for negotiations with Ottawa; and
- an end to conditional grants and joint programs so that the central government would cease to interfere in sectors not within its jurisdiction.

These were the first demands to come from Quebec; and the word demand itself was not used. At most, this was an agenda for future discussion. One cannot resist pointing out that, more than twenty years later, the majority of these demands have been granted:

- At the constitutional conference of November 1981, all the first ministers, with the exception of Quebec's, reached agreement not only on the principle but on the modalities and procedure for repatriating and amending the Constitution.
- Agreement was also reached, again in the face of Quebec objection, on the *Canadian Charter of Rights and Freedoms*.
- A Canadian intergovernmental conferences' secretariat has been in existence for several years; and a federal office of federal-provincial relations and a cabinet secretariat have been entrusted with the responsibility for mapping out the negotiating positions and strategies of the central government.
- An annual conference of provincial premiers has been a permanent feature of the Canadian political landscape since 1960. In particular, it has allowed the provinces of the rest of Canada to harmonize their positions in the face of Quebec's demands.
- The joint programs and conditional grants have indeed undergone sweeping changes. Federal contributions have levelled off and have often been converted into unilateral initiatives.

Only the creation of a constitutional court has not been the subject of an agreement so far, but the issue was not officially on the agendas for the constitutional conferences of 1978–82. This happens to be the only point on which the hopes of the Quebec of the 1960s have not yet been disappointed, and on which there has always been unanimity among Quebec's various political families. Is it just coincidence that nothing has been done in this area?

In a complete reversal of perspective, all Quebec political parties, including the Liberal party, now see the imposition of these reforms as spelling the most significant political defeat Quebec has sustained since 1867. The agenda of 1960 turned quickly into a nightmare.

Premier Lesage's speech at that conference resembled in every respect those previously delivered in the same forum by Premier Duplessis. Detectable in both cases was the predominant influence of the Tremblay Commission's constitutional vision, though neither really made the transition from words to deeds:

> Canadian federalism rests on the sovereignty of Parliament and the provincial legislatures in their respective areas of jurisdiction. . . . For its part, Quebec intends to safeguard the rights and powers conferred upon it by the Constitution [and] to use them fully with a view to promoting the welfare of our population in all matters falling within provincial jurisdiction (Canada, 1960, pp. 30–31; translation).

This statement aroused no controversy at the conference table and prompted no rejoinder. Privately, Quebec participants reminded their Canadian counterparts that the important part of the speech was not this statement of principle but Quebec's determination to put an end to sterile rearguard skirmishing:

> Provincial sovereignty must not be a negative concept, incompatible with progress; it must be a truly living reality, a principle which takes concrete form in institutions and legislative measures. In short, the government of the province of Quebec intends to exercise its full sovereignty in the areas within its competence, though without being unaware that all the governments of our country are subject to an interdependence that is ineluctable (Canada, 1960, pp. 30–31; translation).

These few quotations convey nicely the tone of the first steps in the path of constitutional review. In fact no one, not even Quebec, was thinking in terms of the need to modify essential elements of the Canadian Constitution or the division of powers provided for in it. It would never have occurred to any minister in Quebec City to suggest that this division was an obstacle to implementing the program of reforms. Besides, the majority of these reforms, and particularly those dealing with education and public morality, were concerned only with areas of provincial power. In Quebec City, constitutional interest was limited to the amending formula, which remained the personal business of one minister, Gérin-Lajoie. He soon had many other battles to fight.

Immediately after the conference of July 1960, a system of consultation was set up to put the final touches on the consensus that was thought to have been achieved on the issue of repatriation and the amending formula. Even though no real negotiation had taken place, the participants found themselves with what they believed to be an agreement, probably because none of them, especially not Quebec, gave the subject a very high priority.

Four meetings were held between November 1960 and the end of 1961, and the difficulties surfaced one by one. With each meeting, it grew clearer that this question, in appearance technical and symbolic, could not be the subject of a final agreement. Briefly, three quarrels occurred: first, among the provinces; then between the provinces and the federal government; and, finally, between Quebec and the other governments.

The interprovincial disagreement quickly coalesced around the refusal of Saskatchewan, then led by a CCF government, to accept that every Canadian province should have the right to veto constitutional changes affecting even matters of provincial jurisdiction. At most, Saskatchewan would agree to admit this right for Quebec with respect to the civil law in force there. The Saskatchewan reasoning was actually very simple: the *Constitution Act, 1867* acknowledged Quebec's uniqueness in this one area, but otherwise Quebec was, constitutionally speaking, a province like the others. Giving veto power to all the provinces on the pretext that it had to be given to one of them for a special reason amounted to an admission that there would never be any constitutional change in the country. Besides, at the federal-provincial meeting of July 1960, Saskatchewan's T.C. Douglas had been the only premier to remind participants of the importance of completing the work begun at the constitutional conference of 1950.

During the 1960 conference, Douglas never stopped reiterating that, as quickly as it could possibly be achieved, Canada ought to develop a national policy of economic recovery, a national health insurance scheme, and adjustments to the national unemployment insurance program, as well as increased federal participation in the national system of support for university and technical education. One could not imagine two positions more diametrically opposed than those of the governments of Saskatchewan and Quebec.

Saskatchewan's refusal to allow a veto was not directed against Quebec; it was aimed chiefly at all the other Canadian governments, which were thought to be hostile to the CCF ideology. Paradoxically, however, this opposition, and in particular the pretext it would use, brought out for the first time the idea of a different status that Quebec was supposed to have because certain provisions of the *Constitution Act, 1867* were concerned exclusively with it. It was not so much a Quebec demand as the Saskatchewan refusal which set this process in motion — an odd way for the "Quebec problem" to make its first case.

Ottawa bridled at the growth of this problem of Quebec's hypothetical veto power, which no one had raised before. Nor did the antagonism between a Conservative government losing momentum and the CCF government in Saskatchewan do anything to help. For Diefenbaker, the 1960 agreement in principle marked the end of the project to Canadianize the Constitution. There could be no question of ethnic specificity.

Quebec objected to the formula too in the end, but for very different reasons. Its pretext was the federal prime minister's refusal to give his firm promise to revise a 1949 text which gave the central government the power to amend the Constitution unilaterally in areas of its own exclusive power. The Quebec refusal was primarily tactical, since it was one of a number of ways by which Quebec could reopen the dossier on the sharing of fiscal resources, which had meanwhile emerged as the priority in federal-provincial negotiation.

A Political Season in Canadian Life

In retrospect, it is easier to realize that during all this period Canada had only a very short time in which a certain number of constitutional and political advances could have been achieved, especially on the issues of repatriation, the amending formula, and the Charter of Rights. The period extended from July 1960 to the end of the following summer. By the time of the December 1961 conference, it was probably already too late.

Over these few months, debate was concerned chiefly with points of detail. There was consensus on the basics, and this was all the more promising since it was not the result of a common front of the provinces, or of intense negotiation or compromise. To be sure, none of the participants exhibited wild enthusiasm or made this agreement a matter of political life and death, but the lack of frenzy made for a favourable atmosphere: none of the participants seemed to have a political or emotional stake in the issue. It would never have occurred to anyone to attempt to justify his point of view or settle old scores under such an agreement. In short, there was no question yet of any last-ditch meeting. Agreement was possible because it was not necessary. If it did not come about, this may have been because the need for it went unperceived by either side.

All of this was changed by the federal government's uncompromising position on tax sharing, a position voiced firmly at the October 1960 conference and reiterated at the conference of February 1961. Ottawa refused to make any adjustment whatsoever in the area of succession duties. At the very most, it was prepared to concede a supplementary 6 percent of personal income tax to the provinces. Under the terms of the fiscal agreement, provinces would then be getting 20 percent of this tax. These new arrangements, however, were coupled with a new method of calculating equalization payments, based not on the tax yield of the three richest provinces, as before, but on the average yield for the country as a

TABLE 1-1 Canadian Political Calendar, 1960–61

June 1960	Election of the Liberals in Quebec
July 1960	Annual federal-provincial conference
October 1960	Federal-provincial conference on fiscal policy
December 1960	First interprovincial conference
February 1961	Federal-provincial conference
August 1961	Charlottetown interprovincial conference
December 1961	Federal-provincial conference

whole. The Quebec government's own calculations led it to believe that what it was given with one hand would be taken back by the other.

Had it been possible to resolve the constitutional issue before the fiscal talks reached their intensive phase, or vice versa, it is plausible that an honourable compromise might have been found in each case. Linking the two together in this way, however, meant that failure in one fatally spelled failure in the other. In addition, the fact that the governments were committed to intensive discussion, in order to put the final touches on their consensus, created a political forum which would not otherwise have existed, certainly not in the context of the premiers' annual conference alone. The more frequent meetings made genuine exchanges possible and allowed participants to raise their voices. There was bound to be a verbal escalation.

Reading the reports of these conferences, along with the analyses published in the press, one is struck by the way in which casualness and explosive comments succeed one another in a context that had more in it of theatre than of political negotiation.

One of the main reasons for this false start lay unquestionably in the fact that the constitutional issue had not been the subject of any public discussion at all through 1959 and 1960: there was most certainly no debate on this question before 1962. Anyone in the rest of the country might well ask, and I will do so in more detail in a later chapter, whether there has ever been anything but a series of false starts. In the fall of 1960, however, two seemingly innocuous events — and this is how they were greeted by observers and probably by the participants — would bring a new dimension to the parallel talks on the amending formula and fiscal policy.

These events were the founding on September 8, 1960, of the Action socialiste pour l'indépendance du Québec (socialist action for the independence of Quebec), followed two days later by the creation of the Rassemblement pour l'indépendance nationale (RIN: assembly for national independence). They were added to a third independentist movement, the Alliance laurentienne (Laurentian alliance) which had been founded on January 25, 1957, and which, in spite of the efforts of its leader, Raymond Barbeau, had remained in the shadows. Looking

through the documents of that era again, with the interviews and everyone's memoirs, one finds no special reason for these movements to have
been founded at that exact time. In contrast with 1917 and 1944, there was
no major crisis in the relations between Quebec and Canada. The
recession certainly did not have the feeling of the 1930s crisis.

Competing with one another, their economic ideologies diametrically
opposed, and run by personalities with a lot to say if not much to reason
with, these movements saw their pronouncements suddenly take on a
degree of credibility. The Quebec government's decision to make maximum use of public opinion to get the federal Conservative government
to back down (a government which everyone knew would soon have to
face the voters and which lacked the support it had had in 1958, especially since the defeat of the Union Nationale) had a lot to do with the rise
of the independentist movements.

In fact, when I refer to the Quebec government's decision to make
maximum use of public opinion, I am falling blissfully into one of the
traps which my analysis claims to avoid and which I see as being among
the main stumbling blocks in the way of a clear, if not objective, reading
of the course of events. I am assuming a kind of conscious decision to
proceed in line with a plan of action favouring such an approach. This
way of speaking obviously gives the impression of an unavoidable
sequence flowing from a deliberate causality. However, I am on the
uncertain ground of history that is taking place before our eyes without
the actors being aware of its internal logic. Do they perhaps have the
illusion of awareness?

In 1961 and 1962, the facts that would later be used to prove the
existence of a systematic connection were still very scattered. It is easy
today to make them stand out from the confusion of the times, notifying
us that some prophetic voice, André Laurendeau's or Gérard Pelletier's,
for example, was already proclaiming that more significant realities lay
hidden behind these news items. However, compared with a single
editorial by André Laurendeau, the one of February 20, 1961, in *Le
Devoir*, which qualified as prophecy by recognizing the independentist
choice as a valid one, there were four others that contradicted it or were
simply mistaken, or which simply concerned actual events.

The first RIN demonstration consisted of a parade of automobiles in
downtown Montreal. In March 1961, the daily *La Presse* organized a
home survey on separatism, which gave early militants a chance to
respond en masse. This created the impression of widespread popular
support. This descent of politics into the streets at a time when there was
no election campaign, coupled with easy access to the information
media, was to give these early movements not only credibility but a large
audience as well. Their strength, real or imagined, would then become a
significant weapon in the Quebec-Canada debate. One might speak in
this case of mutual use and an exchange of friendly services. In the first

months of its existence, the RIN was generally content to back the Quebec government in some of its plans and initiatives. At its 1960 convention, for example, the RIN supported the ideas of a ministry of education, a ministry of cultural affairs, and nationalizing electricity.

A Pause

Reviewing the train of events in this period, one is struck by the calm that descended between the months of November 1960 and September 1961. This phenomenon would be repeated later on, as if to confirm that if history has only one destination, it also has many quiet periods.

The Quebec government was completely engrossed in implementing its legislative program and eliminating certain practices which had been dear to the Union Nationale, the replacement of which still required norms to be established, new personnel to be appointed, and decisions to be made on what was to be done with the many skeletons found in the cupboards. What should the government do, however, once it had taken action on certain projects that had been prepared under the previous administration? Of particular importance here were the development of the Manicouagan and the financing of Metropolitan Boulevard, the first urban superhighway in Quebec. What should the government plunge into once the agreements had been signed which civil servants had already negotiated but which the Union Nationale had refused to ratify for reasons of provincial autonomy? This was the case with the agreements on hospital insurance, the Trans-Canada Highway, and forest resource development. What should the next move be after the launching of big commissions of inquiry into housing, the family code, education, and the Labour Code? The government seemed to hesitate about which road to take: it was seeking its second wind.

At the beginning of March 1961, in the first issue of *Le Magazine Maclean* (the French-language version of *Maclean's*), André Laurendeau voiced his misgivings. This generalized feeling seemed to have disappeared completely when it came time to write the history of the period, which came to be seen as a single bloc:

> At times, one had, from the outside, the impression of a slowing down, at the least a hesitation, which was concerned with the objectives and not only with the means. Was the government growing old too fast? (Laurendeau, 1970, p. 5; translation).

As far as the management of federal-provincial affairs went, there was nothing to indicate how important this sector would become. It was only in December 1960 that the services of Claude Morin, then a professor at Laval University, were called on for the first time. His was more of an episodic contribution, however, which was paid for by the assignment and was limited to the writing of the premier's speeches. According to

Richard Daignault, Morin's two greatest qualities were that he produced his texts swiftly and typed them himself (Daignault, 1981, pp. 179–80). During this period, Claude Morin's main speeches dealt only indirectly with the question of federal-provincial relations, a subject for which he had no fondness. His major contribution was to put the new administration's first budget speech into shape: the premier, who was also finance minister, wanted it particularly fleshed out for motives of personal prestige. Thanks to his 92 pages, the goal was reached without any problem.

In his March 1961 diagnosis, André Laurendeau did not linger on the subject. He gave it the same importance as reform of the provincial police. The government's inaction did not particularly stir him up. His only comment was about the fact that Jean Lesage showed equal "flexibility and firmness."

One of the reasons for this relative inattention was to be found in Ottawa itself. In fact, the first skirmishes of a nationalist type occurred on the federal scene, and not in Quebec. These were about bilingual cheques, simultaneous translation in the House of Commons, the national anthem, bilingualism in federal nomenclature, and a distinctive flag. In those days, all these issues looked like a complete waste of time. Quebec City had weightier matters to attend to. Only the minority report of commissioner Eugène Therrien of the Royal Commission on Government Organization (Glassco Commission) contained a more serious analysis.

When in April 1961 the premier wanted Claude Morin to become the first deputy minister in a new Ministry of Federal-Provincial Affairs, Morin refused. A department of this kind looked fairly uninteresting. Federal-provincial dealings were technical in nature, relating exclusively to the fiscal agreements. Given this refusal, the premier appointed Taschereau Fortier, a lawyer and above all a personal friend, to be deputy minister. Fortier died the very night he was to begin, however, and it was thought best not to replace him immediately.

For a long time the ministry was an empty shell, its main job being to prepare for interprovincial conferences, events which had a particularly strong social element, and to take care of management. The fiscal negotiations themselves were still disarmingly simple at this stage, so much so that even the premier could master all the subtleties, which were easily summed up in three figures representing the percentages of the three taxes coming back to the provinces. The responsibility for working out Quebec's position in this area fell to a small group, which consisted mainly of Marcel Bélanger (an accountant acting as fiscal adviser to the premier), Jean Biéler (the deputy minister of finance, inherited from the Duplessis regime), and Michel Bélanger (an economist working as an adviser to René Lévesque).

This account of the condition of Quebec's bureaucracy at the dawn of the Quiet Revolution may seem to be a pointless and anecdotal digression. Clearly, however, the new premier's inability to write his many speeches was an important factor in the establishment of that famous Québécois technocracy. Since the premier also held the posts of finance minister and minister of federal-provincial affairs, and since he thus had to be supplied with speeches on all three subjects, there was a natural coming together of the fiscal negotiation, the practice of Canadian federalism, the constitutional issue (amending formula), and the Quiet Revolution. Under Claude Morin's influence, everything rapidly became material for strategy. His links with the only other team interested in these questions, and the fact that this other team was cheek by jowl with the minister René Lévesque, was not without consequence either.

Obviously, this type of explanation is less uplifting than one that features the Quiet Revolution and the deep strengths of the Québécois people. What would have happened, though, if Premier Lesage had written his own speeches? One sure thing is that Claude Morin would have remained a professor at Laval University.

This approach to the constitutional history of Quebec necessarily raises the question of the place of the little history within the large history. One could always justify this bias in favour of daily life and detail by making references to the "new" history, that of society, mentalities and the anonymous. This would be too easy and also too dangerous, for fashions in history change quickly.

Rather, this bias must be seen as a reflection of my initial hypothesis. The constitutional dimension certainly takes up a growing share of the official record, but the establishment of a new type of relationship between Quebec and Canada was not an essential element in the process of accelerated change that was experienced by Quebec. The constitutional debate is more a mirror that gives back to the Québécois elites and people the image of their new collective identity. Compared with the socioeconomic upheavals, the constitutional business has even a gratuitous look about it.

The Great Turning Point of September 1961

The new political season that began in September 1961 was going to upset everything. In June 1960, the Quiet Revolution and the "Quebec problem" did not yet exist. At most, there was talk of reforms, as becomes any new government, and of disagreements between Ottawa and the provinces, which was certainly no novelty in the political landscape of Quebec.

The rapidity with which events occurred, the fact that one was always encountering the same participants and that a number of them (students, supporters of neutrality in education, pioneers of socialism) finally saw forums in all this for a discussion of issues which concerned them but which had little to do with "the national question," all this helped to

TABLE 1-2 The First Warm Fall: 1961

September 2, 1961	Publication of Raymond Barbeau's book, *J'ai choisi l'indépendance* (I chose independence)
September 5, 1961	Publication of Marcel Chaput's book, *Pourquoi je suis séparatiste* (Why I am a separatist)
September 19, 1961	Union Nationale leadership convention; Daniel Johnson wins
October 1961	Jean Lesage's trip to France
October 1961	First independentist graffiti in Hull and Montreal
November 1961	Congress on Canadian affairs at Laval University with the theme « Le Canada, expérience réussie ou échouée? » (Canada, failed or successful experiment?)
December 1961	Marcel Chaput resigns from his job at the Defence Research Board in Ottawa

convey an image of fevered agitation. The Toronto papers at last discovered Quebec and popularized the expression "Quiet Revolution".

The presence in the separatist movement of numerous individuals who were in close personal and professional contact with the world of federal workers was naturally going to direct the debate toward the treatment Ottawa meted out to the French-Canadians. Marcel Chaput's dismissal by his employer would only accentuate this trend: the theme of the ethnic division of labour, would thus dominate discussion from the outset. It was through the issues of language, French-Canadian minorities, and ethnic relations that the early independentists would popularize their argument.

In a *Le Devoir* editorial of January 20, 1962, André Laurendeau, until then one of the few to enter the debate with the separatists, advised the Diefenbaker government to create a royal commission of inquiry on bilingualism. This was turned down, and in February the Diefenbaker administration decided that its government cheques would be bilingual from then on. The gesture looks ridiculous today. In the papers of the time, demands of this order were the norm.

In June 1962, the federal election left the Conservatives in power, but Quebec returned 26 Créditiste members. This Social Credit breakthrough shuffled the deck considerably. It delayed the Liberal party's taking power, since its only hope of success lay in an almost absolute electoral hold on Quebec. The Liberals, then, at least in Quebec, had to make the Créditistes their chief political adversaries, preventing them from taking the whole field. Between July 1962 and February 1963, when the Conservative government fell, there was a relentless battle between Créditistes and Liberals which centred on the defence of the interests of

Quebec and French-Canadians. On December 17, 1962, when the Créditiste MP Gilles Grégoire tried to grab the headlines at the end of the session, it was by portraying himself as the ardent defender of the idea of a commission of inquiry — even though the notion came from André Laurendeau, one of the fiercest grandstanders on Social Credit. The leader of the Opposition, Lester B. Pearson, had no choice but to fall into step and even to go one better by enlarging, without quite realizing it, the mandate that should guide such a commission (Monière, 1983, pp. 279–80).

In the comment that surrounded the commission's creation, the distinction between language and culture, which was to be so vital later on, drew scarcely any notice. It even seemed that this detail had been added to cushion the shock caused by the idea of a bilingualism commission. Only in November 1963 did Claude Ryan stress, in an editorial, that bilingualism was only the outward face of a profounder reality.

One could not fail to be struck by the change of tone that occurred in speeches by Quebec politicians, and by the premier in particular, between the summer of 1961 and the spring of 1962. By August 1962, at the interprovincial conference in Victoria, Lesage's language had changed entirely. No more was he talking in terms of respect for the Constitution, of spheres of parallel jurisdiction, or of adequate fiscal resources. These Duplessis-style themes had certainly not gone, but they had turned into examples in a reasoning which now, for the first time, came from another direction:

> In the whole of Canada there are approximately 6 million French-Canadians, of whom approximately 5 million live in Quebec. But — and this is an aspect of the problem one can easily forget — we are surrounded by 180 million anglophones who do not speak our language. Yet a healthy realism forces us to look this situation straight in the face and understand that in the interdependent world in which we now live, well-oriented political structures can perhaps allow our people to survive and expand on this territory. In this way the federal government can provide very definite advantages. . . . What French-Canadians are asking themselves today is: "Will Confederation develop in such a way that it will furnish all the guarantees that citizens have the right to call for in the coming years?" (Daignault, 1981, p. 163; translation).

For the first time, the leader of a Quebec government linked Quebec's own destiny to that of the francophone minorities:

> The answer that will be given to this question of Quebec's place in Confederation is connected to the problem of the survival of French-Canadians as an ethnic group. . . . Events experienced on a daily basis force French-Canadians to ask themselves where they are being led by the political, economic, and social direction that our country has taken (Lesage, 1962; translation).

Conclusion Concerning a Dubious Departure

This chapter will no doubt have left the impression that the constitutional debate had trouble taking wing. From 1956 to 1962, in fact, it was nailed to the ground. The Quiet Revolution thus got going without it. Only the question of the amending formula and repatriation, a very secondary element in this affair, was a subject of discussion. Very quickly, however, the consensus worked out among the Canadian governments became the victim of fiscal talks between the two levels of government, as well as becoming the victim of "ways of doing things," this being ushered in by the signing of the agreement on the financing of the universities. Until the winter of 1961–62 there was happy improvisation while the new Quebec government looked for its way. It only found its way the following summer.

This conclusion may seem shocking. It is so only in comparison with the tendency to reconstruct history after the fact, conferring on it a logical causality which the actors of the time could not discern.

It was amid disorder and improvisation that the Quiet Revolution took place. Could it have been otherwise? No society can enlarge the scope of its freedom by following a pre-established plan. We shall thus have to avoid seeing this joyful improvisation as the sign of a lack of seriousness or as a sign of the artificial character of the questions which began to emerge at this time.

Chapter 2

The Marriage of Nationalism and Vote-Getting

If the language of the summer of 1961 already showed a change of tone, this was confirmed by the November 1962 election. As we now know, this election had very little to do with the nationalizing of electricity, at least as far as the voters' decision was concerned (Pinard, 1969). Its significance lay elsewhere.

An Election Out of the Ordinary

It was certainly not its constitutional content that made this election important. In this respect, the Liberal platform was even less overblown than it was in 1960, containing only a solitary phrase on the subject: "To assert Quebec's role in Confederation." The questions of Quebec-Canada and federal-provincial relations were barely touched on in the platform. This lack of interest stemmed in large part from the reasons we gave in the previous chapter (Lesage's past history as a federal politician, the ambiguity of Liberal positions, and distrust of nationalism). To these must be added the close ties that still bound together the two Liberal parties, which were in fact one and the same organization. It was only in 1965 that the break-up was sanctioned, and then not without difficulty.

Beyond these structural reasons, it is important to mention the political personality of René Lévesque, who was not only less than interested in federal-provincial matters but was actually suspicious, still associating them closely with the rearguard actions of the Duplessis era. When the cabinet embarked on an intensive discussion of the nationalization project, the nationalist component played a very secondary role. The debate took shape more in terms of left-right, province-Montreal, progressive-traditional, and public-private.

Nationalist themes were not absent in the election campaign, but it was more a question of what one would describe today as economic nationalism, or the nationalism of affirmation. At no point was there mention of Quebec's place in the Canadian federation.

In spite of the significance generally attached to it, this election was not won by the Liberals as massively as one might have expected from a party that was riding an unprecedented wave of popularity, led by a "team of thunder" and in symbiosis with a population thirsting for change. A few weeks before the balloting, internal surveys by both parties pointed to a tough battle. To turn the scale to the Liberal side, it took the twofold gift of a televised debate, won hands down by Premier Lesage, and a false scandal involving voters' cards. A survey by the Groupe de recherches sociales (1962), which was carried out on the eve of the election, showed how little Quebec public opinion had evolved during two years of Quiet Revolution.

The very decision to run an election on the theme of the nationalization of electricity was made almost by accident as the result of an eleventh-hour suggestion from Georges-Émile Lapalme:

> It is Mr. Lapalme himself, as René Lévesque tells it, who had the idea of combining it with an election. And everyone rallied around quickly on that. It came point-blank. It arrived, for most of us, like a clap of thunder. Then, very rapidly, from instinct, people told themselves, "Yes, that makes good sense." As for me, my feeling was, "This is going to be a bloody good chance to stage an economic campaign. We've never had that in Quebec." Others may have had an idea that this would give new élan to the party. I don't know about that. It's possible. I am sure this had to work in some minds, because it was an eminently popular subject at the same time (Provencher, 1973, p. 188; translation).

In contrast to the previous campaign, this one was organized with the help of communications specialists, who naturally gave a prime place to television and to certain favoured themes. Obviously, we should not accord these people all the importance, but neither should we let ourselves be fooled by the false distinction between form and content. In deciding to give Jean Lesage the image of a chief of state, which fitted well with his somewhat pompous oratorical style, and in deciding to make maximum use of the talents of René Lévesque, as well as maximizing the use of certain words (such as *Québécois* and *State of Quebec*), the producers unquestionably had an enormous influence on the public image of the campaign (O'Neill and Benjamin, 1978).

We know today, from the research, that it was more the general image of a government which was organized — which knew where it was going and had a plan — that was the determining factor in the vote, and that it was not necessarily the nationalist content of the government's messages. In 1962, broadcast messages of national identification were still very rare and they were far from being as effective as some liked to believe. The failures of KEBEC beer and La Québécoise cigarettes are there to remind us of this (Elkin, 1973). The fact that the first public-opinion polls contained no questions on respondents' ethnic identification or national orientation speaks of the little interest these issues sparked at the time.

In more than one respect, this campaign was a true stroke of election genius. It allowed the government to repair its unity, which was a trifle threatened by the patent ambition of certain ministers to implement reforms that were so far simply clauses in an election platform, if that. All the fall-out from the revelations concerning the former government could be used to advantage, putting the Union Nationale in an unflattering light and thus getting around the fact that the majority of the population alternated between unconcern and incredulousness about the frequently exposed old practices. There was also the hope, after the election, of bringing some new faces into the government and of getting rid of certain symbols that were in the way, including George Marler, the representative of anglophone business circles. Although a member of cabinet, Marler had difficulty expressing himself in French.

Another stroke of genius, if ever there was one, was the campaign theme. By promising to bring the Hydro-Québec project to completion, the government was making a fairly direct pitch to Union Nationale supporters and to all who remembered the deals surrounding the creation of the Action libérale nationale. René Lévesque did not invent the logic of the struggle against the power companies, but he knew how to channel the feeling for use in building a modern state — something at which the traditional, apolitical nationalism had never been successful. Besides, the simple theme of the nationalization of something could not be seen other than favourably by the contingent of new voters coming along in 1962. Finally, it was a stroke of genius because this theme made it possible to get the rest of the province embarked in the movement of the Quiet Revolution. It is too easily forgotten that although the 1962 election campaign in Montreal relied heavily on the slogan of "Maîtres chez nous" (Masters in our own house), coupled with collective self-affirmation and economic reconquest, what carried the day elsewhere in the province was the assurance of seeing hydro rates brought down to the level charged by Hydro-Québec in Montreal. In the lower St. Lawrence region, the rates were 93 percent higher than Montreal's (Jobin, 1978, p. 56).

This election showed clearly the enormous popularity the themes of modernization, affirmation, and economic development enjoyed with the people who defined the situations. The grouping of themes under the umbrella of the economy would increase the credibility of the new nationalism. At that time, as today, there was much disapproval of the drain of time and energy caused by national struggles. The newspapers and magazines were bristling with appeals to take care of the real problems. The opposition of the magazine *Cité-libre* is remembered best, but other magazines (*Liberté*, *Parti pris*, and *Révolution québécoise*) were not in favour of the national struggle either, at least not in the form that the nationalist movements, old and new, aspired to give it.

From this moment on, complicity and close ideological connections would unite the members of the government and the media. This election campaign, with its oratorical excesses and with the escalating demagoguery on both sides, took the theme of "control of one's destiny" to heights never reached before. The campaign would also push into the limelight one minister who, although an important member of the "thunder team," was still only an equal in the group. Up to this point, Georges-Émile Lapalme and Paul Gérin-Lajoie had tended to monopolize a great deal of attention, the former because of his cultural affairs ministry and the latter through educational reform. The nationalization election would change everything.

This election was decisive for the later development of the political society of Quebec. It gave the government a respite of 30 months before the next vote, and there is reason to think that the need to hold an election in June 1964 would have prompted the government to much greater prudence in its reforms, or else that this would have brought about the government's fall two years sooner than actually happened. In fact, in 1964 the debate was raging on the creation of the Ministry of Education, and in its April budget the government was forced to standardize some consumer taxes upward (sales tax, tax on spirits).

An Unexpected Result

The election's repercussions on the Union Nationale were no less significant. During the campaign, the Union Nationale's new leader used up a considerable amount of energy going after every little aspect of the socioeconomic policies of the party in power. It was all there: non-denominational schools, tax hikes, the communists, the new patronage, the neglect of agriculture and socialists driving out business.

Its ensuing defeat at the polls forced the Union Nationale to rethink its approach completely. Above all, it had to find a new wrinkle in what was beginning to be known as the "national question," since in the end, or so the party thought, this was what had made it possible for the Liberals to hide all the cracks in their administration. For Daniel Johnson, the thing to find as soon as possible was a theme as powerful as the nationalization of electricity. For tactical reasons, the party decided to pass the Liberals on the road of nationalism.

Here, it is essential to understand the party's situation in the wake of bitter defeat. It was ruined financially, and most of the staff had to beg private business for personal grants to cover their salaries. A party of cadres if ever there was one, the Union Nationale had lost most of its organizers, as a result of four reversals since 1959: the deaths of Duplessis and Sauvé, and the defeats of 1960 and 1962. Such a traditionally structured party could not long survive three leadership campaigns and four leaders in three years.

The divisions within the party were so numerous that one hesitates to check them off: between supporters of Jean-Jacques Bertrand and Daniel Johnson, between the old guard and the newcomers, between the nationalist wing and the federal Conservatives, between the supporters and detractors of John Diefenbaker, between the urban and rural elements, and between Quebec City and Montreal. To escape from these tensions a little, Daniel Johnson took refuge in study trips to Europe. At the end of 1963, many party members were convinced that another change of leadership was inevitable.

The Catholic hierarchy's about-face on Bill 60 for the reform of education would further aggravate dissensions in a party that was losing its only trump:

> If the high clergy themselves agreed to the loss of a large part of their influence on teaching, it was hard to see how a political party could set itself up as the defender of the Catholic Church! Daniel Johnson, who had not been informed of the cardinal's intervention in the debate, had just learned another political lesson. You cannot be more Catholic than the Pope! (Gros d'Aillon, 1979, p. 66; translation).

In the fall of 1964, the party held a special caucus at Mont-Gabriel, where Daniel Johnson was forced to promise that general sessions would be organized for the next year to work out a political philosophy. It was only by this manoeuvre that he averted an explosion. In the following months, Johnson made a few speeches on the constitutional issue, but his proposals often had no purpose beyond scoring off the premier or scoring off Johnson's own adversaries in the party. This was how he came to talk about the need to go beyond the repatriation of the Constitution, simply to differ from the government position on a question which, in the beginning at least, generated neither interest nor animosity. The idea of a constituent assembly is due to Johnson's wish not to support the proposal for the holding of an estates-general; even though this was an official element of the party platform, it had the misfortune to be Jean-Jacques Bertrand's pet project.

The Opposition leader, constantly looking for allies and trying by all possible means to break out of the isolation in which the caricaturists had confined him, met increasingly with whatever Quebec had in the way of groups and grouplets. For them, Daniel Johnson and his party were a useful springboard and no more. According to Pierre Bourgault

(1983, p. 149), the leader of the Opposition set so little store by the political shadings between his party and the RIN that he apparently offered to make an official alliance on the eve of the 1966 election! All this was in order to stay afloat and beat the Liberals on their own ground.

It was only a few weeks before he summoned the 1965 sessions that Daniel Johnson (realizing that his party, which still lacked a coherent position, had at the most a few piecemeal statements) asked staff members to provide him with a well-padded document. This was to be *Égalité ou indépendance*. The genesis of what would become a rallying point for all Quebec nationalism and would officially consecrate the myth of Daniel Johnson has been described by Paul Gros d'Aillon in terms that leave one somewhat perplexed:

> In Montreal, I had a call from Johnson. He seemed a bit embarrassed. The day before, during a squabble in the House, the leader of the Opposition had upbraided the premier for beating around the bush on constitutional policy. The latter, stung to the quick, had warned Johnson that he planned to publish the full texts of his speeches on this question and that anyone would be able to see that his position had not varied. Daniel Johnson too had made numerous statements on the question of federal-provincial relations and he had decided to steal a march on Jean Lesage by issuing a condensed version first (Gros d'Aillon, 1979, p. 88; translation).

One can easily imagine a new biography of Jean Lesage or the memoirs of Claude Morin coming out one day to reveal that on the same evening Lesage, realizing that he had gone a bit far and panicking, asked his adviser to draw up a clearly defined position. Perhaps Lesage suddenly changed his tone in order to have a rejoinder for the resplendent new position of the Opposition leader — a position that was better established than the government's.

On being told by Johnson, "I am having you sent all the texts. See what can be done with them and give me an answer on the weekend," Paul Gros d'Aillon set resolutely to work:

> By the next Sunday . . . I had reread all the texts of his statements on the constitutional question and noted that there had been, over the years, a steady development in his thinking. From the straightforward special status that was one of the initial themes of his constitutional theory, Daniel Johnson had come to the concept of equality within a binational Canada, and this proposition now had the tone of an ultimatum. It was not simple to bring these scattered and necessarily fairly diverse fragments together into one whole. A new impetus, on the other hand, would make it possible to go farther. . . . In a week, the basic document was ready. . . . But a conclusion was needed for the little book that hurled a scathing charge at the present federal system. . . . The book finally closed with these words: "Canada or Quebec, wherever the French-Canadian nation finds freedom, there its homeland will be" (Gros d'Aillon, 1979, p. 90; translation). A careful reading of Daniel Johnson's speeches and statements leads one to

conclude that this idea of a progression in his constitutional thinking is not supported by the facts. Before the publication of *Égalité ou indépendance*, for example, he had never actually spoken in favour of special status for Quebec.

For Daniel Johnson, this represented a complete and virtually instantaneous reversal in attitude, and it was dictated by partisan realities. As so often happens in the political game, he was caught in the trap of his own words. Forced to argue the merits of his position with his eternal rival, Jean-Jacques Bertrand (who was even more suspicious of nationalism than he was), Johnson came to feel more and more at home in his Quebec-nationalist skin, and he was all the happier when he received a good dose of admiration from journalists and opinion leaders, especially those of the student movement, who had previously made him their star scapegoat and had saddled him with the nickname of Danny Boy.

The transformation of Daniel Johnson had begun, and if we can say that the 1962 election created René Lévesque, progressive nationalism, and the Quiet Revolution, we must also add to this list the name of the future premier, Daniel Johnson. It is no slight to his memory to note that his constitutional thinking developed largely in contact with political reality. Why should we be surprised that a politician could decode the new political environment so handily?

In its way, Johnson's realism was proof of the vitality and growing autonomy of the political system at that time: Daniel Johnson and the others who followed could only recognize this.

The Government's Handling of the National Question

In November 1963, talks reopened on tax sharing between the new Liberal federal government and the provinces. Quebec called for the division to follow the formula of 25-25-100 percent: 25 percent of personal income tax, 25 percent of corporate income tax and 100 percent of succession duties. The logic of parliamentary opposition prompted Johnson to suggest that anything under 100-100-100 percent would spell a major defeat for the Liberal government. In the end, only 18-9-75 percent was obtained, but Lesage promised to return to the charge in March 1964, when the federal-provincial conference would look at the question again. In the meantime, tactical requirements told Jean Lesage to raise his voice, and this he did bluntly.

During this interval, talks also began on two other questions, the pension system — one of the Pearson government's election promises — and federal withdrawal from the joint programs. It would be of interest here to illustrate the by-play among the three negotiating tables in greater detail. On May 16, 1963, for example, Pearson called stalemate for the first time with his plan for a universal pension scheme; Lesage replied with an ultimatum on the tax-sharing issue, which prompted Pearson to suggest a federal-provincial conference, and his Quebec counterpart agreed.

At the same time, May 1963, Jean Lesage travelled to Britain, where Quebec had just sent its first delegate. On his return, he gave a ringing speech at the University of Western Ontario for which there seemed no motive, except perhaps the next federal-provincial conference:

> If ever Confederation broke up, it would not be because Quebec, the political expression of French Canada, separated; it would be because they did not know how to keep it (Larochelle, 1982, p. 57; translation).

While the premier was reacting in terms of the federal-provincial agenda, Johnson's actions were guided by what Lesage did as well as by the internal tensions wracking his party. The result was an escalation of statements and proposals from anybody and everybody. Nor was there a lack of forums for self-expression. In addition to the various sessions of the interprovincial and federal-provincial conferences, the summer of 1963 saw the launching of the parliamentary committee on the Constitution that included Jean Lesage, Daniel Johnson, Paul Gérin-Lajoie, Georges-Émile Lapalme, Jean-Jacques Bertrand, and René Lévesque, for whom this was the first experience of the area. The committee secretary was Claude Morin. In July, the federal government created the Royal Commission on Bilingualism and Biculturalism.

At the meeting of July 1963, which presumably was called to discuss fiscal agreements and the pension scheme, a quite different subject was canvassed in the end: federal aid to municipalities. At the March 1964 conference, at which Jean Lesage had promised to return to the charge with the 25-25-100-percent formula, the final agreement reached was on federal financing for municipalities. Although Ottawa could finance the municipalities, Quebec saved face, since the sums earmarked for municipalities would be administered by the provinces. In the legislative assembly, Daniel Johnson could only lash out at this treason by the Liberals, who used the opportunity to boast about the merits and especially the profitability of their approach. This was, however, a carbon copy in every detail of the agreement on university financing.

At the same time, the pension system was discussed. The haggling that enveloped these negotiations is well known, and although it can doubtless be attributed to the sincerity and intensity of the participants, one cannot resist, with a 20-year perspective, smiling at the theatrical aspect of the whole affair. How could anyone actually have believed that "Canada was in danger of exploding before Easter" or that the country had come within an inch of disintegrating? Can anyone think for a single moment that Jean Lesage would seriously have suggested the secession of his province for Quebec taxpayers to foot a supplementary tax entitling them to a state pension one day? Any politician can cultivate a pronounced taste for electoral suicide if he wants, but never to that extent.

In the summer of 1964, agreement finally came on the pension scheme and the joint programs at the same time. Quebec then found itself with 44 percent of personal income tax. The legend was born of a great victory for Quebec. An image of Canadian federalism took shape as well, that of a pendulum swinging dangerously to the side of the provinces. This image would be crucial later on, which did not prevent it from deviating seriously from reality. I shall come back to this later.

Let me repeat, the point here is not to return to criticism of these agreements, under which the provinces, on a basis of punctuality, obtained the fiscal resources which let them carry out some of their constitutional responsibilities, in return for which they agreed to federal participation and also to a certain number of working principles that would come to haunt them later on. It came, then, to be accepted that:

- the quality of a provincial program depends entirely on the existence of so-called national norms, and that the more these norms are applied fully and equally at the level of the entire country, the more the program is judged to be satisfactory;
- any federal-provincial agreement must be based on the existence of and respect for these so-called national norms, even if the program is administered directly by the province and falls within its jurisdiction; and
- there could be no federal-provincial programs except in areas of provincial jurisdiction (wholly or partly).

In offering these few conclusions — which, I agree, could be explored further — my purpose is not to prove the alleged perfidy of Ottawa which, by these agreements, succeeds in keeping political victory from Quebec, the only player to lend itself honestly to federalism. Rather, the point is to emphasize that the notorious weakening of central power, which all observers and most participants like to report, has not really happened. Canadian federalism is thus not the sacrificial lamb among the other federal systems, which, in contrast to Canada's, have centralized considerably since 1945. As we will shall see in a later chapter, Canada has mainly become less concentrated since 1960: it has not truly decentralized and even less has it regionalized, as some are pleased to note and above all to deplore. Such was the assertion, however, that all involved felt obliged to make in 1965.

During the crucial years of 1964 and 1965, the Liberal government stuck with a clever approach that combined appeals for change with threats and analyses of failure. Although this may mean attributing to governments an overcapacity for thought, one would be tempted to conclude that in these years the Quebec government seemed obsessed with the search for the best possible negotiating position, never missing a chance to discredit the adversary and put him on the defensive. It forgot, however, that true political power is measured only when the potential for using it exists. This is how we have to interpret Quebec's refusal to accept the 1965 (Fulton-Favreau) amending formula.

Rereading the reports of the period, one discovers the extent to which the Quebec-Canada negotiations were only a secondary objective, one way among many to let Quebec's awakening find expression.

Formula Trauma

The story of the Fulton-Favreau formula speaks clearly of the Quebec government's relative lack of interest in this whole question. It was in June 1964 that Prime Minister Pearson suggested a fresh attempt to find an agreement on the amending formula at the coming federal-provincial conference. The fact that Saskatchewan's CCF government had been replaced by a more amenable Liberal regime, and especially Pearson's preliminary discussion with Quebec, encouraged him to believe that the long-sought goal would be reached at last. Quebec's good will was due entirely to its need to show flexibility and receptiveness to compromise while talks on subjects considered to be far more important were going on.

They decided in Quebec City to take full advantage of the centennial mystique that was beginning to stir around Ottawa. Beyond an obsession with finishing before 1967, there was nothing to require the governments to reach agreement rapidly on the amending formula. In this regard, the situation was very different from that of the reconstruction period, when such a change was seen as essential. Having agreed "in the Canadian way," in particular on the pensions and unemployment insurance, the governments no longer felt the same urgency. Only the frequent upsets on the political chessboard could explain these repreated attempts to reach an agreement when no one was convinced any longer of its absolute necessity. From 1957 to 1963, deaths and elections changed one or other government in office in Quebec City or Ottawa every six months on average. Each time, the need was felt to seize on the new situation and get the file closed.

In the summer of 1964, an initial agreement was reached among the provinces, and it was made official at the Charlottetown federal-provincial conference in September. On October 30 the definitive text of the amending formula was published, and two weeks later Premier Lesage assured his federal counterpart of his intention to have the formula accepted by his legislative assembly during its January session. Thus, only two weeks passed between the final agreement and the premier's letter. It seems that the cabinet cast only a symbolic glance at the document and that no one thought of laying its contents before the parliamentary committee on the Constitution that had been struck the previous year.

No serious evaluation was made of this formula, still less of its effect on public opinion. Besides, it was at the time of this debate that Jean Lesage let fall his unfortunate phrase about the uneducated. When the nationalist opposition made the argument that the formula would block any change in the Canadian Constitution to accommodate the new aspirations of Quebec, there was genuine surprise among the members of the government, who were working at top speed in ground operations which aimed at retrieving administrative powers and a greater fiscal autonomy from Ottawa. The notion of using the constitutional route to make these results official was altogether foreign to government strategy, although one could not really speak of strategy.

When, to its surprise, the government discovered that it had to obtain the approval of a legislative council that was dominated by the Union Nationale, panic reigned. At the last minute, it was decided to take the route of an address to the Queen, enjoining her not to give effect to the refusal and counter-appeal of her legislative council. In March 1965, René Lévesque was deputed by the premier to defend the formula before an audience at the University of Montreal. Thinking that he could get through by improvising, he was met by boos from the students and by jeers from his opponent, Jacques-Yvan Morin. This cold shower would have its influence on later events as well. For the first time, René Lévesque, the darling of the student body, was put in a minority! The humiliation would prompt him to ask for a change of assignment and in particular would force him to take a closer interest in the constitutional questions, which he had more or less neglected up to then, being satisfied, like all other participants in the great spectacle of the Quiet Revolution, to utter a few telling phrases, whenever possible before anglophone listeners or in Toronto.

This would be the Liberal party's first and last foray into the field of constitutional reform. The defeat, the first for the Liberal government, did not prompt any real thinking about the party's position, or rather about its lack of a constitutional position. The government more or less froze in anxious immobility. The attitude was not peculiar to the constitutional area but was encountered during this same period in all other sectors of government activity. The 1966 platform was drawn up without system on the basis of individual suggestions from a few ministers, and was collated hurriedly into a document that bragged of past achievements. A glance at the various ministerial proposals shows that only Pierre Laporte had given a place of importance to the Constitution.

Premier Lesage's lengthy journey to the Canadian West in October 1965 had the effect of another cold shower on any impulse toward constitutional change he may have had. This was his first sustained contact with a body of English-Canadian opinion that had the increasing sense of being pushed aside and left in ignorance of what was really happening in Quebec. In this regard, there can never be enough emphasis on the devastating effects the early incidents of political violence had on any image people could have had of Quebec. Here, these events were arousing a curiosity that was amused and sometimes sympathetic. They did not escalate or spread geographically, to the keen disappointment of the FLQ. Reactions in the rest of the country were quite different.

Everywhere, Lesage received a chilly welcome. Yet his message made no mention at all of special status for Quebec or of any far-reaching rearrangement of the division of legislative powers. Essentially, he confined his remarks to the mutual respect due one another by the country's two great cultures, and to the rights of the francophone minorities and bilingualism in the federal civil service. In the letter he wrote on his return, informing Prime Minister Pearson that Quebec could not give final acceptance to the Fulton-Favreau formula, he offered a very clear explanation of the reasons that prompted him to reject any initiative in the constitutional area:

> The visit I made recently to the Canadian West caused me to become aware of the difference between the way Quebec would like to see our constitutional system develop and the views on this subject of a number of Canadians in the other provinces. . . . I consider that we should give everyone a sufficient space of time to reflect on the country's future. . . . By then, I imagine that each government will have had an opportunity to define its policies, not only in the area of federal-provincial relations but also regarding relations between French-Canadians and English-Canadians (quoted in Roy, 1978, p. 66; translation).

In 1966, other events helped relegate the Liberal party of Quebec to a background role: the crossover by Pierre Trudeau, Gérard Pelletier, and Jean Marchand to the Liberal Party of Canada, and the summoning of the estates-general.

In March 1966, the Federation of St-Jean-Baptiste Societies brought to Montreal the representatives of twenty or so groups working in the area of culture and education. Within a few months, 12,000 groups had been contacted, 103 meetings called, and 1,026 delegates selected. Given the vacuum left by the government, interest turned rapidly toward this huge and well-oiled machine.

The Liberal party's loss at the polls in 1966 left it in a state of shock. A reading of the detailed reports of the many post mortem meetings held by the party right across the province indicates that very few members attached any importance whatever to the issues of the Constitution or Quebec-Canada relations when analyzing the causes of defeat. Except for René Lévesque, no one in the party undertook to think about this element of the program. The publication of his manifesto on sovereignty association on September 18, 1967 took everyone by surprise. His party had no alternative position to offer. At the outset, the party leaders were not even able to make sense when faced with this realignment plan. It was only after forceful denunciations from Senator Maurice Lamontagne and Eric Kierans, the president of the Liberal Federation of Quebec, that the opposition mobilized.

A rejoinder was drawn up post-haste. It contained a condemnation of "separatism in all its forms," a "formal" recognition of the two Canadian nations, a statement favouring minority rights, and a plan for a constitutional tribunal. Obviously, the Liberal party no longer had the inside track. The triumph over the Lévesque set was short-lived. Some time later, the three instigators of Réne Lévesque's departure — Jean Lesage, Eric Kierans, and Paul Gérin-Lajoie — all left the Quebec Liberal party.

At the same time, the debate was moving elsewhere, to the estates-general of French Canada, which held its sessions on November 23, 1967, and to Ottawa, where the Royal Commission on Bilingualism and Biculturalism was publishing the first volume of its official report on December 5 of that year.

One might have expected the Liberal party to make the constitutional and national issue its top priority, with claims on its resources and energies. Such was not the case. The choice was to handle it purely in terms of politics, if not simply of elections. Why? The answer to this question does not lie in the simple internal dynamic of the party. The fact is that no one actually asked the party to formulate an answer.

The Quiet Improvisation

The anxious improvising of the Liberal government was succeeded by the fortunate improvising of the Union Nationale. Daniel Johnson was slow to get involved in the fight against the Fulton-Favreau formula. It was only after a few sorties by the constitutionalist Jacques-Yvan Morin, and in despair of ever finding a base from which to attack the Liberal leader, that he plunged into the fray:

> At last Daniel Johnson had found the flaw in Jean Lesage. He assessed the situation clearly: the premier's unconditional support for an amending formula which made the future of Quebec subject to the veto of English Canada. . . would isolate him from the nationalist and intellectual elements that had sustained him so far. Lesage's blunder threw the doors of power wide open for him. . . . The sterling opportunism which, seeing the enemy exposed, seizes the advantage to deliver the K.O., gave meaning to Johnson's impassioned battle (Godin, 1980, vol. 2, p. 25 and 26; translation).

If this sterling opportunism produced good results, the reason was not so much the accuracy of Johnson's analysis as the fact that his strictly partisan stance managed to mobilize support from a number of groups whose motives for joining the movement varied enormously. For the RIN, which had only just decided to become a political party, it meant a longed-for chance to rise to the level of the recognized parties by campaigning with the leader of the official Opposition. For the students' movements, whose backing would be important, it was a matter of making the government pay for its arrogance on the *Samedi de la matraque* and speed up negotiations on the bursaries and official recognition for the movements. For the Créditistes in Ottawa, it was essential to maintain their image as champions of the rights of French-Canadians.

For the members of the Union Nationale, the fight against the Fulton-Favreau formula and the "equality or independence" program began simply as happy diversions to take attention away from the party's internal disagreements and its lack of any alternative solution. They were quite willing to fraternize with the most nationalistic elements of the Quebec intelligentsia, but they were also determined to keep this friendship platonic.

In fact, at the very moment when Daniel Johnson was getting ready to take power, his attitude remained the same in every respect, whether on the great reforms of the Quiet Revolution or on the federal-provincial squabble. Opportunism, ambiguity, and a disposition to wait and see were its essential elements. This is how a biographer, even one whose palm was crossed in advance, has characterized the Johnson style:

> For Daniel Johnson, there were two kinds of matters: the ones that ironed themselves out with time — pointless to get involved in them — and the ones that were not ready, in which case the wait-and-see approach applied (Godin, 1980, vol. 2, p. 366; translation).

There could be no question of taking Johnson to task for his caution and for his refusal to jump into adventures. It should be borne in mind, however, that this prudence was not accompanied by any medium- or long-term strategic view. At times, this wait-and-see philosophy resulted in substantial shifts in ideology. I have already mentioned how Johnson moved over from special status (in theory, at least, since the facts do not corroborate this, but no matter, he thought so) to the idea of associated states and "two nations."

It has to be stressed at this point that once Johnson was in office and sitting at the table for constitutional talks, we would hear no more of the plan for a confederal constitution that was supposed to be topped off by "a truly binational body where the delegates of the two cultural communities could work, on a basis of equality, to manage their common interests" (Johnson, 1966, p. 109; translation). Nor would anything more be heard of the constituent assembly or the referendum that was to complete this process.

There is some risk in casting doubt on the constitutional performance of Daniel Johnson, who, thanks to a measure of political transubstantiation that would not have fooled the man himself, has emerged as the preeminent Quebec statesman. With regard to Daniel Johnson's style and strategic abilities, however, Pierre Godin's reading encourages one to conclude that here, at the very best, was theatrical improvisation so vacillating that it convinced no one and ended up by looking like an awkward spectacle on the rink.

IMPROVISATION

Johnson assigned the development of strategy for Quebec to a working group made up of the technocrats C. Morin, J. Parizeau. . . . For the technocrats it was arduous work. To C. Morin, who asked him to shed some light on the matter, Johnson replied: "Read my book, *Égalité ou indépendance*, and you will understand where I'm going." Morin followed this advice but was still puzzled. Attentive and repeated readings of the Gospel according to St. Daniel did not lead to a clear understanding of his boss's constitutional position (Godin, 1980, p. 302; translation).

THEATRE

Johnson negotiated like a union leader. He began by threatening and asking for the moon. He had understood for a long while that the idea of separation scared the anglophones, and he never failed to give it a flourish. . . . But once at the negotiating table far from his nationalist public, the tiger became a nice little pussy. . . . Used to Lesage's bluster, the provincial leaders were delighted to find that tiger Johnson had paper teeth (Godin, 1980, pp. 303 and 304).

HESITATION AND CONFUSION

(After the failure of the fiscal conference of 1966)

First he had to defuse English Canada. Some journalists had come down in favour of independence a little too soon, Johnson maintained. . . when getting off the plane. "I am seeking the equality or independence of the French-Canadian nation, not Quebec. It is not the same thing. . . . One hundred percent of direct taxes is one thing. Equality is another thing. Equally, independence is another thing. Some people have come up with the following equation: one hundred percent equals equality and, if there is no hundred percent, it's independence. In reality, these are three separate things" (Godin, 1980, pp. 306–307; translation).

PERMEABILITY

(At the time of his convalescence in Hawaii)

During these long hours of idleness, Paul Desmarais managed to persuade the premier to effect a strategic withdrawal to reestablish the confidence of Anglo-American business circles in Quebec. . . . Before finally agreeing, he wanted to do a last check. From his *cabana*, he reached Paul Dozois, who once again gave him confirmation of the hysteria in the business community. He forgot to inquire, however, at the Caisse de dépôts [deposit fund], where Jacques Parizeau observed no abnormal dealing in Quebec government bonds (Godin, 1980, pp. 269–70; translation).

Once he pulled back, Daniel Johnson's lack of real interest in the whole business of constitutional review was easier to discern. What held his attention more was the theatrical setting it gave him for projecting a different public image and rebuilding his party. Daniel Johnson's grand design was not to make Canada over on a binational basis but to make the Union Nationale a modern party in step with the new Quebec.

The fact is that the Union Nationale government was one of the worst champions that Quebec's cause had had since the dark days of Adélard Godbout. Daniel Johnson's death and the election loss of 1970 seemingly let this fact be covered up. The utterances were flamboyant, the aims praiseworthy, but the government could never decide whether it was going to Ottawa to negotiate a new constitution, to reform the present constitution, to discuss joint programs and tax agreements, to drive a spike into *Cité-libre*, or to engage in dialogue with the other Canadian nation.

In every sense, the results were catastrophic. At the time of the federal-provincial conference on the division of the fiscal pie that was held in Ottawa in the fall of 1966, the new Quebec premier met with a brutal response from Mitchell Sharp, the federal finance minister. Sharp did not feel it was necessary to wait for the arrival of Pierre Elliott Trudeau to put Quebec (and the member for Bagot) in its place.

When one looks in detail at the events of 1966–68, it is hard to sort out the mistakes which were purely technical and those which revealed an absence of strategy and serious thinking. Whatever the case, the result was the same.

Not wanting to be outstripped by the most nationalistic elements in the party or to provide a forum for the independentists and René Lévesque, Johnson put an immediate stop to the work of the parliamentary committee on the Constitution, which finally disappeared in 1968 after waiting 17 months for the government to call it in. The failure of this committee is a good illustration of the difficulty that both governments, Liberal and Union Nationale, ran into with the handling of a constitutional debate in which they could see nothing but the constraints of party and the dates of elections. Is there cause for surprise that the debate slipped increasingly out of their control?

The idea of having this parliamentary committee was put forward in May 1963 by Jean-Jacques Bertrand, who saw it as an effective means of embarrassing the Liberal government and scoring off a leader who was thought at that time to be incapable of pulling himself together, let alone his party. In Bertrand's mind, one of the committee's jobs would be to make the arrangements for the estates-general so that the people could decide what political status was fitting for Quebec. Through Paul Gérin-Lajoie, the government voiced its objection to so sweeping a mandate, and it was then agreed to focus on "the objectives to be pursued by French Canada in the review of the Canadian constitutional system."

From its beginnings, this committee annoyed the lawmakers considerably, and it is surprising to note the gap between the high quality of the research and briefs presented to the group and the poor uses to which they were put. In all likelihood, the committee's survival was due essentially to the hard work and skill of its secretary, Claude Morin, who was alone in his conviction that the constitutional talks being called for so loudly would lead nowhere without preliminary work on a political synthesis. This work was never done.

From March 23, 1963, to December 2, 1966, the committee had 16 meetings of which 13 were spent listening to papers on the various constitutional options. Spread over so lengthy a time, the meetings lacked the critical intensity that could have sparked true, thoroughgoing debate. Every time the committee met, the process had moved on a little, a federal election had rearranged the chessboard, there were new faces around. Discussion began again from scratch. Change affected relations among committee members and their positions in their respective parties as well. None of the members felt that it was necessary to take an active part in working out a process and defining a research program. No systematic effort was made to convince recalcitrant groups to come forward with their briefs. University groups, labour unions and municipalities all missed the call.

No one believed that the committee was for real. It was freely admitted that the body was mainly a forum for the nationalist and independentist groups to spread their ideas. No one really needed the committee, especially not its members. These included three future premiers, all of whom had numerous places to express themselves and not the slightest intention of getting involved in teamwork on a topic so close to their political sensibilities and careers.

On the whole, Daniel Johnson took no constitutional initiative, unless in agreeing to take part in some conferences. It was Ontario and its Premier Robarts that called the first constitutional meeting, the Confederation of Tomorrow Conference, which was held in Toronto during November 1967. In spite of Johnson's very active presence at the meeting, backed by a well-prepared team, he had little real influence at this conference. Since Quebec had not been able to help with the agenda, all it could do was react.

Ontario was again the first, through its Advisory Committee on Confederation, to put an exact idea of Canadian federalism on the table. To be sure, this committee would have little immediate influence on the development of government positions, but it would manage to present some synthesis of the options and issues in dispute — a success which always eluded its Quebec counterpart.

At last, the federal government, the great absentee at the Toronto discussion, picked up the ball by calling, for February 1968, the first session of a constitutional conference that would meet under its chairmanship until February 1971.

The Quiet Trample, 1968–70

Even when the constitutional conference met for the first time at Ottawa in February 1968, it was hard to imagine how Quebec could hope to come out a winner. The only element in doubt was the date and precise extent of the ultimate defeat. This did not become clear until 13 years afterwards, and it was total. In this sense, the failure of the constitutional conference of November 1981 was not chiefly the fault of the negotiators of the Parti Québécois government — even though their behaviour at this last stage cannot be passed over in silence. All the governments of Quebec, as well as those of Canada, must share the blame, as must the Quebec elites and English Canada as a whole. This was one of those exceptional cases when a defeat was not actually an orphan!

Until 1967, the initiative in discussion rested with the Quebec government and with all the Québécois definers of situations. This is the sense in which the widely heard statement has to be understood, namely that "without Quebec, there would have been no constitutional crisis." This was true up to 1967, but less so beginning with 1968 and the arrival of Pierre Trudeau, and not so at all in 1973, with the eruption of western Canada and economic issues that had been accumulating since 1964. This whole period is distinguished by a slow marginalization of Quebec, which ceased to have a special voice, this being for a number of reasons, some of them fortuitous (changes of government and premier) and others more structural (energy crisis, economic decline).

Beginning in 1968, the federal government understood the political interest it had in dominating the constitutional debate. It was not afraid to use the agenda, timing and substance of the debate for political ends, following the lead of the Quebec parties in 1960–66. It seems that the lesson bore fruit. Here, it is important to grasp all the refinements of the position of Quebec when it attended the conferences in Toronto (November 1967) and Ottawa (February 1968). This position was seen by all involved as extremely unstable, and indeed it was.

In the space of two years, the Government of Quebec had changed its constitutional strategy at least three times. In 1964, the Liberal government agreed to satisfy Ottawa on the priority search for an amending formula, since it hoped to get advantages from this in terms of fiscal policy and the joint programs. The next spring, this strategy was discarded under pressure from opposition to the Fulton-Favreau formula. The government then decided to freeze the entire constitutional issue. With the coming of the Union Nationale government, the strategy changed again, since priority was given to the constitutional review, which Quebec would try to turn toward official recognition of the "two nations."

In the fall of 1966 there was another abrupt change. At the September 14 federal-provincial conference on fiscal policy, Daniel Johnson returned to the charge on sharing the pie. It was agreed to put the constitutional demands on the back burner in order to obtain more tax points. For this purpose, Quebec tried to revive an interprovincial front, which seemed to have all the more chance of success in that it confined itself to money questions in which the other provinces had similar interests. In addition, this priority on fiscal matters was completely consistent with Ontario's approach.

Given Mitchell Sharp's inflexible attitude, Daniel Johnson decided to alter the Quebec strategy yet again and bring back the constitutional debate, this time with a different approach. However, we can no longer really speak of strategic choices; instead, we should talk of a decision, conscious or not, to play on all the tables at once. As a result, Daniel Johnson applied himself during this period to:

- making use of forces which, in his party and in Quebec, were pushing toward constitutional radicalism (Godin, 1980, vol. 2, p. 307);
- reviving the historic Quebec-Ontario alliance;
- isolating Ottawa by means of an interprovincial common front;
- reviving the potentially explosive front of the French-speaking world, with the more than active complicity of Charles de Gaulle (Godin, 1980, vol. 2, p. 307);
- defusing the bomb of independence to reassure English Canada (Godin, 1980, vol. 2, p. 305); and
- reassuring the financial community and using its support to prove his good faith.

Only one strategy is lacking from this moderately ample list:

- reaching agreement with Ottawa at any price, against the rest of Canada if need be, and with the active complicity of the new federal team.

Apparently, this last is a strategy that none of the Quebec parties, need I say, ever planned to put into practice. To come into existence, a Union Nationale-*Cité-libre* front would have required more than just a breakdown of its strategic value! As for the Quebec Liberal party, it had burnt all its bridges in 1965 when its two wings, federal and provincial, made their divorce official. The appearance in Ottawa of a new Liberal team, recruited in large part outside traditional Liberal circles, was to complete the break.

We have already turned to the personality and style of Daniel Johnson to explain this mania for accumulating strategies without ever eliminating one. The dynamic of party relations in Quebec and the tensions within the party have also been tapped. There is another factor that is not very conceptual, which ordinarily prompts me to neglect it: the state of Premier Johnson's health. This raises an exceptional but nonetheless real situation affecting recent leaders of Quebec and Canada. In our present case, the political story was coupled with a medical story which partly explains it.

In early September 1967, Premier Johnson experienced several heart problems just as he was beginning some important talks with Alain Peyrefitte, the emissary of the French president, concerning the sequel to General de Gaulle's recent visit. The message from de Gaulle was clear:

> In the financial, economic, scientific, and technical sectors, my government will be immediately in a position to offer specific proposals to your own concerning our common effort. With regard to culture and education, Monsieur Peyrefitte, to whom I entrust this letter, will indicate to you what the Paris government is ready to do right away, which is quite considerable (Godin, 1980, vol. 2, p. 258; translation).

This was a handwritten letter sent directly from Poland, where the French president was on a state visit. Few governments could boast of having received such an offer of services. The letter has remained in the Johnson family archive, and the premier himself never mentioned it publicly (Lescop, 1981). It throws new light on the so-called mystery surrounding General de Gaulle's visit and the meaning of his famous words. In fact, the mystery existed only in Quebec, knowingly fostered by none other than the premier. In Paris and Ottawa, the interpretation was not a matter for doubt.

The negotiation with the French minister took place in the Hotel Bonaventure, where Premier Johnson was under medical supervision and where the seriousness of his condition could be more readily concealed. It was an ill premier, cut off from his cabinet colleagues and advisers, who talked with the French envoy. In the end, there was retreat right down the line. Johnson kept nothing from the French offer, but he could only reap benefits from his refusal since he was still counting on French support and the effect this offer would have on nerves in Ottawa. The two confined themselves to raising the credits for cultural and technical exchange, providing for ministerial meetings, and laying the basis of the Office franco-québécoise de la jeunesse (France-Quebec youth bureau). Of political cooperation there was none. They went as far as to avoid officially signing an agreement, in order to leave no room for criticism. It is not known what remarks Peyrefitte made to the French president on his return. Yet one can imagine that such a reception definitely put the brakes on a potential Paris-Quebec axis. To the French, it was now obvious that the premier's days were numbered and that he was using France for his federal-provincial manoeuvring. They were not wrong.

In the three weeks that followed, Daniel Johnson had to seek refuge in Hawaii for a forced vacation. Paul Desmarais and Marcel Faribault, the president of General Trust of Canada, went with him and convinced him of the need for a complete change of attitude. Another two weeks and it was the Confederation of Tomorrow Conference, in Toronto; the premier arrived in a fresh state of mind. One understands better now how other participants got the impression of dealing with a tiger in public and a kitten in private.

Again his illness prevented him from following the proceedings attentively after the first session of the new constitutional conference, which was a trifle stormy. This lack of interest would make it possible for the federal government to deflect the flow of the debate completely. When Premier Bertrand found himself at the negotiating table for the February and June 1969 session of the constitutional conference, he would be without allies, without a fallback position, without objectives, and with no solid proposals to offer. In addition, he would be in the middle of a leadership race, since the party had not recognized his authority immediately. A worse negotiating posture cannot be imagined.

Daniel Johnson was never specific about what content he envisaged for his concept of political equality between the two nations, simply reiterating that this was self-evident, that even the Royal Commission on Bilingualism and Biculturalism saw the necessity of it, and that it was the only bulwark against separatism. For the premier to keep to generalities in the period before the constitutional conference was good diplomatic warfare; but when, afterwards, he kept to remarks just as vague and went as far at times as to do an about-face or to stop referring to them, this was thoughtlessness.

Daniel Johnson's illness and death prevented him from giving the full measure of his talents as a negotiator. Yet, it is hard to see how his approach could have differed from that of his immediate successors. Once the process of constitutional review had begun, the result which came in Victoria seemed inevitable. In that negotiation, the personalities or politics of Quebec's representatives were not a determining factor; that role fell to the attitudes and relative strengths of the two other actors in this mini-drama — English Canada and the federal government.

A Dangerous Thaw

The arrival of Robert Bourassa as premier of Quebec spelled a complete break with all the strategies put forward by Quebec governments since 1965. The new premier chose to differ on each of the points that had typified his predecessors' approach:

- Whereas Lesage, Johnson and Bertrand had talked about a process of constitutional review extending necessarily over several years, Bourassa made it clear, as early as the September 1972 session of the constitutional conference, that he wanted to get results rapidly.
- Contrary to his predecessors, he chose to attend to constitutional

matters personally and to stake his entire prestige and reputation on them.

- He recognized that the criterion of effectiveness alone must direct the development of a new division of legislative powers.
- He defined the objective of the whole exercise of constitutional review from a strictly Canadian perspective, namely to "preserve and develop the bicultural character of the Canadian federation."
- He agreed to keep to the seven topics formally on the agenda since 1968: official languages, basic rights, division of powers, reform of the Senate and the Supreme Court, regional disparities, amending formula, and procedures for federal-provincial relations.
- He agreed to limit the Quebec government's special responsibility to the sole sector of culture.
- He withdrew from his vocabulary all formulas liable to offend the other governments or to be misread by them: Québécois nation, national government, special status, founding peoples, equality.
- He agreed to negotiate and reach agreement with Ottawa and the other provincial governments on an amending procedure before concluding an agreement on a division of powers.
- He chose to limit his legislative claims to a special sector, namely that of social affairs.
- He announced his intention of reaching administrative agreements that could replace a constitutional agreement.

We shall never know whether such a reversal could have borne fruit. One thing is certain: the October Crisis arrived to disturb everything and completely overturn the logic of Bourassa's compromise.

It was enough, in fact, that events put the federal government in a dominant posture for Bourassa's wager to be lost even before the game began. Every one of the elements of strategy just listed would turn against its author in the end. For example, in September 1970 the decision to make the premier directly responsible could have looked like a careful strategic calculation. In the case of success he would have taken all the glory, and in the case of failure there would have been no reason to blame him. In fact, failure would actually have strengthened his position with a number of nationalist groups as well as at the inevitable fiscal negotiations to come. The whole strategy rested on the theory of the first six months to which the premier had subscribed straightaway: "It is in the first six months of his mandate that a newly elected leader has enough margin for manoeuvre to deal with the unsolvable problems." The first six months were indeed determining.

The October Crisis, its unfolding, and its ending would contribute to the premature aging of this government while rapidly taking away any advantage its momentum could have given it. In September 1970, it seemed as if it could be blamed for nothing and praised for everything, while a year later it could be blamed for everything and praised for nothing. This is exactly what happened.

To gauge the extent of Quebec's defeat, it is enough to read the news analysis from the day after the "no" of Victoria. In Quebec, Bourassa was given no credit for political vision on account of the refusal. Rather, it was said that popular pressure and certain more energetic ministers prevented him from committing an unpardonable blunder. In the rest of Canada and in Ottawa, he was the villain of the piece. The wording of the Quebec government's refusal also shows the weakness of the position in which the premier had put himself, and which was accentuated by this rejection:

- The refusal is embedded in a statement of unshakable faith in the virtues of federalism.
- There is no reference to the special place that Quebec should occupy at the heart of the federation. At the most, there is mention of the need for Canadian federalism to "reflect the diversity of the regions of our country."
- The constitutional review is judged satisfactory in terms of rhythm, substance, procedures, and results.
- No reference is made to any feeling of urgency whatever or to the need to get somewhere.
- Quebec's requirements and traditional approach are not reaffirmed.
- The reasons for the refusal are limited to a few uncertainties that have not been cleared up in terms of security of revenue.

The day after this historic "no" looked deceptively like the day before. Nothing had happened and nothing was happening. On the other hand, something could have happened; and around this hypothetical future, seemingly it might have been possible to mobilize Quebec. As the ex-minister Claude Forget has often said, this ability to say no is absolutely one of the privileges of all national minorities.

Always the Same Conclusion

In Chapter 1, I tried to bring a little demystification to the source of what is known as "the Canadian political crisis." Getting off on the wrong foot, Canadian constitutional reform could only develop into a series of deadlocks which needed heroic efforts to break them.

The time has come to put these grandiose visions of the constitutional process in their place before they are embedded permanently in our collective folklore. Fortunately or unfortunately, depending on one's point of view, the reality is less exhilarating than the technicolour vision in which all the actors, winners and losers alike, have leading parts which they count on playing again at the earliest opportunity.

There is no question here of moving to the opposite extreme and arguing that this result was the product of chance, or that the Canadian negotiators showed understanding and that the Quebec ones showed competence; quite the reverse. Quebec's constitutional defeat was too real to be passed over in silence. The result can be seen as one that was desired, sought, and obtained, because when things came right down to it, there was no attempt to get the talks back on the right track. If there is to be talk of conspiracy, it was a conspiracy of mediocrity, a conspiracy that succeeded because of important errors of judgment on the part of the Quebec negotiators.

Whereas Chapter 1 tried to show that the constitutional process was not injected into the Quebec political debate until late in the day, and even then superficially, I wanted in this chapter to spend some time on the train of events. Since this 1966–75 period saw the first big manoeuvres of constitutional review, the Confederation of Tomorrow Conference, and the "no" of Victoria, it has inevitably monopolized attention. Everything has already been said about these events and where they led (though this will certainly not prevent it being said all over again). I have thus dwelt only briefly on the events of these heady years, choosing to bring out a few points which are usually ignored but which deserve to be stated at least once.

I shall now confine myself to a few observations about the beginnings of this famous constitutional debate:

- The political and electoral history of the period 1956–62 reveals no demand for change in the framework of the Constitution or in Quebec-Canada relations.
- The two major political parties and their new leadership teams were barely concerned about these questions.
- Election considerations were what allowed the constitutional question to blight the political landscape of Quebec.
- The increase in forums for political debate, along with the tactical requirements of federal-provincial negotiations, were determining variables in terms of generalizing the debate.
- From the outset, the constitutional issue was an integral part of the political activity of Quebec parties, without any attempt being made to develop a consensus or common opinions on the subject.
- In the official meetings that brought representatives of English Canada and Quebec together during this period, there was no real discussion of Quebec's status, of potential constitutional formulas, or of Quebec-Canada relations. The Government of Quebec showed no more interest in a frank debate of the question than the federal government or the other provincial governments did.

Quebec's referendum would allow it to regain the initiative in the debate. It was, by its very wording, a confession of weakness for which Quebec alone would be asked to pay the price. In appearance, at least.

Chapter 3

"Over and Out"

Following the passage of the *Constitution Act, 1982*, it was relatively easy to view this act as a plot, worked knowingly by the rest of Canada, to "put Quebec back in its place" and make it pay for the years of bickering. There are in fact several indications to lend credence to this view; but if we look more closely behind the ringing assertions, we find several of the mythic visions that were mentioned in Chapters 1 and 2.

The extent of Quebec's loss inclined one to think that this *Constitution Act* was more than a common accident, that it could only have been the product of sleepless planning. Did not the fact that the sense of defeat was shared by the supporters of both sovereignty association and renewed federalism speak of the scope of a loss which could only have been organized, since in Quebec it left none but losers in its wake? For the two sides, this reconciliation in defeat came too late. The constitutional agreement in fact signalled the end of an objective that was shared secretly by both: Canada's reconstruction on the basis of political equality between the two collectivities, in order to get Quebec out of its minority and provincial status once and for all.

For the sovereignty group, the *Constitution Act, 1982* spelled failure for the very concept of sovereignty association, not so much by the act's substance as by the process and play of forces that had produced it. How could there be association if English Canada refused even to acknowledge the existence of a distinct political collectivity?

The disappointment was no less keen for the proponents of renewed federalism, who could have had serious hopes of seeing their ideas used as a basis for future constitutional discussion. After its referendum victory, the federal government hurried to pass the *Constitution Act, 1982* without really asking their opinion or, worse still, waiting for them to get back into office. This could only mean a fixed resolve in the rest of Canada to reject any notion of different, particular, special, or national status for Quebec. In the federalist camp, of course, they used prudence before handing out blame too severely. They also carefully avoided learning any lesson whatever from the rout, ascribing its authorship solely to the leaders of the federal Liberal party. The fact that not one Quebec federalist learned the lessons that were imperative after this episode is a revealing indication of the quasi-mythic value attributed to federalism: it became a kind of sacred value in itself, not to be challenged without bringing down the wrath of ancestors.

On the other hand, a good number of sovereignty supporters did seem to have learned something from the recent events. The sovereignty thesis no longer had quite its old fetish value. Tactics, strategies, and basic options were put up for review amid an intellectual ferment which some read as confusion. There was still some way to go before reaching a better understanding of the true state of Quebec affairs, but the process had begun. Unfortunately, the same could not be said of the federalist forces. Regrouping under the Liberal party banner, they had decided to wait for the winds of power to blow again.

Beyond the customary recriminations about "the discourtesy of the federal Liberals" and mention of the inevitable personality conflicts, there was no analysis of the situation worth having. The slap administered by the federal government was even advanced as proof of the provincial federalists' good faith. In their minds, the only purpose of the entire repatriation effort had been to prevent the province's Liberal party from gaining power. All these labours had been motivated solely by the desire to stop that dangerous Quebec nationalist, Claude Ryan, from becoming premier and effectively combatting the federal coup.

This is an interpretation of great heat and interest, as are all interpretations of this type. At one time or another, we all give in to them, and why not?

By the familiar process of compensation, Quebec's political elites had come to explain so sweeping a defeat in terms of the plotting and connivance of their enemies. Of course, the two ideological families did not have quite the same definition of these enemies or their motives, but the diagnosis was basically the same: the plans for seriously reforming Canada's political framework had been rejected because they disturbed English Canada. Both sides had greatly underestimated the capacity for resistance, both active and passive, of the federal state and the social and economic forces it controlled. Since that state was only a caricature of American desires, they had thought it would be relatively easy to change, forgetting that the caricature corresponded fully to the aspirations of the majority of anglophone Canadians. Even a semi-state can turn out to be extremely tough.

This view of things found its counterpart, and some welcome confirmation (in certain explanations that were current in the rest of the country) of the other conspiracy, that of the Parti Québécois negotiators, who were presumed to have been waiting for the right moment to scuttle the constitutional talks — grist to their separatist mill.

Must I again stress the irony of these two diagnoses, which in both cases depended on the existence of national attitudes and behaviours? It is only when they get together on labelling one another with the darkest intentions that the country's two national collectivities consent to mutual recognition. In these circumstances, is it really worth the trouble of cutting through the protective isolation around our two solitudes?

"We'll Talk Another Time. . . . Over and Out"

So there was supposedly a general conspiracy. Everyone seemed to have done his part: the federal bureaucracy, the Parti Québécois, Pierre Trudeau, the anglophone premiers. A real conspiratorial happening! All were guilty: the Parti Québécois, which could not defend Quebec's interests as it ought because it did not really believe in the process; the federal Liberals, who were more concerned with maintaining their privileges than with giving Quebec federalists a place in the sun; and the provincial Liberals who did not know how to rally behind their leader.

However, the previous chapters have tried to show that if there was conspiracy it was relatively recent. Never under Lesage, Johnson, Bertrand, or Bourassa had Quebec really presented a relatively united position; relatively, for we delude ourselves if we think that unanimity is possible on the subject. To the cacophony of voices was added a medley of strategies, tactics, and goals that were adjusted to suit election dates and party realignments. In short, Quebec may have known what it wanted, but it never expressed it with a single voice. This was never a real priority.

We can deplore this, but should we be surprised? Can a democratic society speak with a single voice? Even if it wished to, it could not marshal the means. Under the Duplessis regime, and in 1917 and 1944, as well, Quebec could have its unanimity. It is always easier to build consensus when the choices are limited, the stakes kept low, and the avenues of expression all but nonexistent. In the 1960s, however, the Quebec political arena had suddenly become a place of power, decision, and confrontation. In this context, one could not expect to keep the constitutional question away from party crossfire.

Taking a different view of the story as it unfolds in its first phase (1957–71), one has the impression of an implacable mechanism following a logic of its own. The mistakes of Quebec governments seem intent on piling up, while the central government can wait until its Quebec partner is winded, changes, or simply finds itself in a position of weakness; no need to conspire when patience is enough. This is the patience that is inseparable from the inertia of all political systems, which means that aside from revolutions and other moments of madness, important political changes are spread over generations rather than popping up in last-ditch conferences.

Is it worth the trouble to keep telling this story? What use is there in going back to the recent details, especially since they are known and since the rest could already be guessed after the first two acts? If I do continue, it is out of concern for continuity, of course, but also because this last episode contains some supplementary lessons. In particular, one will learn that the federal coup of the autumn of 1981 had very little to do with the Parti Québécois victory of November 15, 1976, or the Quebec Referendum of May 20, 1980. The supreme irony here is that the PQ played only a very secondary role in the constitutional burial of Quebec!

Those Forgotten Years

It is usual to think of the years 1971–76 as a kind of constitutional lull. The significance of the election of November 15, 1976, seems to have relativized everything before it to such a degree that certain events appear to have been dredged from the course of history. The defeat of Robert Bourassa has helped banish memory of the speech he gave at the time, about the imminence of a serious constitutional crisis and a major political confrontation between Quebec and Ottawa. Rarely do losers manage to impose their view of history, let alone of the events that procured their defeat. It is easier to retain the winner's version of the reasons for his victory than the tortured explanations of the loser.

The history books do not seem to have remembered 1975 as one of the key years in recent political and constitutional development. The years 1976 or 1978 are preferred. Nevertheless. . . .

Although recent constitutional history is alive with theories about the smallest move by every player, one can only surmise what reasons may have prompted Pierre Trudeau, in April 1975, to make a fresh attempt to reach agreement on the amending formula. No province had asked for it. When the report of the joint Senate and House of Commons committee on the Constitution was tabled in the House, it showed how much everyone's feelings on the subject had hardened. Re-elected in 1974, the Trudeau government was still years away from an election campaign. In short, there was no pressure to open this Pandora's box again.

Only the prime minister's personal attachment to the ideas of repatriation and a charter of rights can account for this return in force. The energy crisis and the dizzying rise of inflation may add up to another plausible explanation. These events could have persuaded the federal authorities of the need to get new economic powers as quickly as possible.

This absence of a specific motive explains in large part the casual handling of the whole effort, at least until November 1976. The process degenerated rapidly into unprecedented federal-provincial confrontation when Ottawa's intentions became more visible.

In a speech of April 20, 1975, Prime Minister Trudeau told Liberal party members that Ottawa had not the slightest intention of parting with the legislative powers it had in the cultural area.

Three weeks later, at a federal-provincial conference on communications, Cabinet Minister Gérard Pelletier said that the same stipulation applied to communications, especially the cable sector. In October 1975, the federal government announced its program of wage and price controls.

These events did not, of course, pass unnoticed at the time. In Quebec, however, the Liberal government decided to view them merely as the temporary problems of what was generally called "cooperative federalism." Battling with an independentist opposition which refused to let up, Premier Bourassa could not recognize that here was something that represented more than a few mishaps which could be dealt with by private talks or by some interprovincial common front. In the 1960s, Quebec premiers had been able to come to terms with independentist movements operating outside the national assembly, but Robert Bourassa did not have the same latitude. In this connection, one cannot resist pointing out the vast manoeuvring space always enjoyed by the federal prime minister in his relations with Quebec and the other provinces.

Begun in this climate, the constitutional negotiations would have difficulty coming to an all-parties agreement, especially as there seemed to be no urgency to push them ahead. In fact, these were not negotiations in the strict sense; rather, they were a series of bilateral consultations between the central government and each province, to sound out its plans and expectations. This approach was a complete reversal of Ottawa procedure. Rather than holding a meeting of civil servants and ministers or premiers, it dispatched Gordon Robertson to "gather the opinions of the provinces." Here was the hallowing of the federal monopoly on the process and substance of constitutional reform.

Even though it could have flatly rejected this new approach, especially when this was seen to go hand in hand with unilateral initiatives and the open intention of carrying on in the same vein if necessary, the Bourassa government merely stated that there could be no repatriation of the Constitution unless the new constitutional text included adequate guarantees for the protection of the French language and culture. Was this a conscious move, or was it a product of negligence, a bureaucratic slip-up such as occurs so often in all governments? The fact remains that this response would allow Ottawa to speed up its pace.

Not only did the response amount to tacit acceptance of Ottawa's modus operandi, but the stipulation with it (even when compared with those voiced in the preceding round), marked another retreat. Instead of taking the initiative, the Bourassa government merely reacted to the federal initiatives and was thus reduced to asking if the new constitution would restrict Ottawa's powers of unilateral intervention. This Quebec stance shows just how far things had gone since 1967, when Quebec was demanding a new constitution that would give it more powers. This time, Quebec was so far gone as to request a new constitution whose main function would be to oblige the central government to respect the old constitution! In agreeing to private negotiation, the Bourassa government doomed itself to continually having to define and defend its own position, without being able to require the same of its partners. When it entrusted the middleman role in the constitutional dialogue to one of the important protagonists, if not the most important, Quebec diminished its own role still further.

The consequences of this tactical thoughtlessness were disastrous for a negotiating Quebec whose position was not particularly promising in any case. When Quebec had informed Ottawa of what it meant by "constitutional guarantees to French culture," Ottawa undertook to put these demands into shape and to distribute them to the other provinces. This was done in a letter dated March 31, 1976, a letter that was very unusual in the tradition of constitutional bargaining. In it, Trudeau expressed his own reservations about the new federal proposals:

> As I mentioned, it was Mr. Bourassa who laid down the principle of the "constitutional guarantee," a condition essential for him. Sections 38 and 40 attempt to respond to the questions raised by his representatives. Mr. Bourassa knows that these sections arouse some concern in my colleagues and myself, and he is well aware that it is up to him to justify them to his counterparts in the light of the situation of the French language and culture in Canada (Roy, 1978, p. 293; translation).

This was a direct invitation for the premiers to reject the proposals. Remember that, two weeks earlier, the prime minister had delivered one of his most memorable speeches, clearly announcing to thousands of worked-up supporters his intention of not letting the nebulous concept of cultural sovereignty torpedo constitutional reform again.

The March 31 letter was clear about the federal government's determination to go ahead, with or without the consent of the provinces. By burning all his bridges behind him like this, Prime Minister Trudeau made certain that his plans would have to go ahead. The day after sending this letter, he tabled a document in the House of Commons which summed up a potential federal defence in the courts in case the provinces objected to his unilateral move.

There is no doubt that Ottawa fully intended to act unilaterally. This is what it ended up doing, by following the exact scenario described in the letter of March 31. Given the agitation of the provinces, a new letter dated October 18 advised them as follows: that their opposition was useless and without foundation; that their attempt to put the question of increased provincial powers on the agenda was a waste of time; that only the question of the amending formula would actually appear on the agenda; and that any federal-provincial conference on these questions would be a pointless digression.

Never had a federal prime minister been so clear. In contrast to the situation of the 1960s, when in spite of deadlock on the constitutional front, agreement was always possible in the area of the joint programs, this time the federal government refused all concessions on the other issues in dispute. To use an expression from labour relations, we could speak of a stiffening both at the central negotiating table and at the sector tables. This moment marked the death of cooperative federalism.

The Constitutional Correspondence

The election of the Parti Québécois would force the federal government to change its opinion, but solely on this last point. This was the context in which the 1978–80 negotiations were conducted. Contrary to what is so often said, this round of negotiations was in no way a response to the election of an independentist government.

In the pre-negotiation phase, which lasted from 1975 to 1978, the federal government tried every means of getting control of the constitutional agenda, and for this purpose it used the possibilities offered by correspondence with the provinces, sometimes collectively and sometimes individually. For their part, the provinces tried to coordinate their activities from time to time. The exchange of letters which typify this period are most revealing:

- On October 19, 1976, Prime Minister Trudeau replied to a letter from Premier Lougheed of Alberta, who had written to him after interprovincial meetings in Toronto and Edmonton. Trudeau expressed his lack of enthusiasm for the process of an overall review of the Constitution, which the provinces were unanimous in wanting. He preferred to stick to repatriation and the amending formula.
- One month after Lougheed's letter was sent, and thus after Trudeau had replied, Premier Campbell of Prince Edward Island suddenly changed his mind and wrote to tell Trudeau that the Lougheed letter did not really represent the position of his island, which wished to stick to repatriation (November 10, 1976).
- Just as the provinces had embarked on intensive consultation after Trudeau's reply, he wrote to them again, on January 19, 1977. Pleading the need to clarify his thinking, he announced that Ottawa no longer objected to enlarging the discussion on the basis of Lougheed's proposals, provided that anything affecting the division of powers was excluded for the time being. This letter also offered some specific details about the substance of what Ottawa wanted to send to London.

Whereas the former proposal had mentioned only the cultural guarantees insisted on by Bourassa, the new text included provisions on the Senate, regional disparities, language rights, and equalization.

It is essential to grasp the full significance of this letter. After the provinces had expressed their disagreement with the idea (not the substance) of proceeding only with repatriating the Constitution and had then suggested broadening the process to include the division of powers, here is Trudeau replying to them (having made sure, meanwhile, that their common front was not holding), and saying that he was ready to go ahead in line with one or other of the following formulas: proceeding according to the initial plan, though this time it would include more than in its first version; or proceeding according to an expanded formula, though on condition that the item the provinces were really committed to, the division of powers, was excluded. Very skilfully, he gave them the choice between going ahead with a modified version of their agenda or with a new version of his program. In either case, the result would be the same: discussion of the subjects seen as priorities by Ottawa, and avoidance of those that were important to the provinces.

- As in the case of Trudeau's first letter of October 1976, this January 1977 letter brought a response from the premier of Newfoundland, Frank Moores, who wrote that his province must now reexamine its whole position to take Trudeau's offer into account.
- In a letter dated February 15, 1977, one week after the letter from Moores, Premier Lougheed informed the new premier of Quebec that he no longer felt entitled to reply to the federal government in his name. He suggested that each premier respond to Trudeau directly. This marked the official end of the common front.
- No further exchange of letters took place until June 1978, some 16 months later. Trudeau had ended his last letter, of January 19, 1977, by asking the provinces to make their views known to him on the "present proposals" and especially on the "next stage, in order to put the final touches to the repatriation process." Nothing more specific was mentioned in terms of deadline. In the meantime, the front of the stage was taken up by the court rulings on the Quebec cable and Saskatchewan potash cases. In the summer of 1977, the federal government launched its task force on Canadian unity, which confirmed the general impression that Ottawa had decided to wait before proceeding with its plans.
- On June 12, 1978, the federal government tabled its white paper, *The Time to Act*, and on June 20 it brought in Bill C-60. The two documents were totally different and had very little connection with one another, in contrast to the usual function of white papers. *The Time to Act* was nothing but a lengthy plea for Canadian federalism. Quebec was passed over in silence, or, rather, it was reduced to the role of a region

in the Canadian cultural mosaic. As for Bill C-60, it proposed an extensive overhaul of the federal framework, but in a way that would increase the powers of the central government. To give only two examples, s. 39 provided that the Parliament of Canada would alone be able to decide on the creation of new provinces, a move backwards from Victoria, and s. 98 made the federal government's declaratory power official.

The door had closed, then, compared with 1975. Starting out with the intention of putting into the Constitution what the governments reached agreement on in Victoria, the federal government ended up several stages later with a proposal for constitutional reform which perceptibly increased its own powers, which gave satisfaction on one or two points to each of the English provinces, and which did absolutely nothing about the claims of Quebec. Even Bourassa's rather timorous demand for a commitment "to guarantee the safeguard and development of the French language and the culture of which it is the foundation" was altered to a commitment to a "Canadian *francophonie* concentrated in, but not limited to, Quebec."

This was the situation when the 1978 constitutional discussions began.

The Negotiation and Its Dangers

According to one of the most widely held views, the Quebec government was not particularly interested in serious negotiation with its Canadian partners between 1976 and 1980. It is even supposed to have done all it could to make these last-ditch talks inconclusive and thus prove to the Quebec voters that independence was now the only way open to them. The same argument would be used about the post-referendum phase of the constitutional negotiations. It is probably too late to change this perception. Too many of those involved have reasons to maintain this thesis for it to disappear so easily. For the Liberal party of Canada and the provincial governments that were signatory to the November 1981 agreement, the advantages of this post facto rationalization are obvious. For the Progressive Conservative party, it is both an alibi and a weapon in potential negotiations with Quebec. As for the Quebec Liberal party, the argument props up the claim that the Liberals can do better than the Parti Québécois.

As is often the case with such interpretations, this one rests on some facts. For one thing, it is correct to state that the Parti Québécois government was not the most active of the negotiators in this period. It was not trying to find a compromise at any price. The main reason for this was not so much a desire to scuttle the talks as the impossibility of getting these negotiations to focus on the subject of Quebec's demands.

In the summer of 1978, the minister of intergovernmental affairs had a negotiating brief prepared which rehearsed in complete detail every demand for constitutional change ever voiced by a Quebec government. When this document was put on the discussion table, it aroused no comment whatever. It was greeted by absolute indifference. Moreover, no provincial delegation ever referred to it. In private conversations, no request for more information was ever addressed to any member of the Quebec delegation. All attempts to get other delegations to react to the document failed miserably. (This is an ironical twist when one realizes that, before its publication, certain Quebec ministers expressed fears about the possibility that the other Canadian delegations might jump on this document and decide to make it the official position of the Government of Quebec.) Given this indifference, which verged on contempt, the lack of enthusiasm in the Quebec delegation was understandable, as was the delegation's decision not to take an active part in the discussion on topics as important as the monarchy or divorce.

If we grant that this indifference to Quebec's positions, like all the other examples of indifference, was not necessarily the product of a conspiracy or of a determination to distort reality, it must also be granted that it was proof of a profound ignorance about the Quebec political situation and about the goals which were pursued — in a very incoherent fashion, as I have often said — by the various governments that followed one another in Quebec City.

One of the most astonishing things, seen across the years, is the considerable energy and resources that the Quebec government did devote to the constitutional review process between 1976 and 1981, as much for the interprovincial as for the federal-provincial gatherings. Solely for the meeting of provincial premiers in Regina in August 1978, the general directorate of federal-provincial affairs in the intergovernmental affairs ministry assembled a support package of several hundred pages, under no fewer than 16 headings. Under a number of these headings, of course, there were only exchanges of correspondence or draft statements, but the package also contained analyses and highly detailed negotiating positions. Among these documents were:

- a descriptive analysis of 46 pages entitled *La révision constitutionelle: Rétrospective 1867–1978*;
- an analysis of the progress of the constitutional debate since 1975;
- an 11-page analysis of the federal document *The Time to Act*;
- a judicial analysis of the provisions regarding rights and freedoms contained in the federal proposals;
- a study of the principles underlying *The Time to Act* and Bill C-60;
- a comparative analysis, some 30 pages long, on the Victoria proposals, those of 1976 and Bill C-60;
- an annotated press review of cross-Canada reactions in the wake of Bill C-60;

- comparative analyses of current Quebec positions and interprovincial compromises;
- a summary of the previous positions of the elected Parti Québécois members between 1970 and 1976;
- an annotated summary of all correspondence exchanged since 1976; and
- a detailed analysis of the provisions in Bill C-60 regarding a new Senate.

Of all the provincial delegations, Quebec's was unquestionably the best prepared, or at least as well prepared as Ontario's. Even a passing acquaintance with those responsible for Quebec's dossier, coupled with a minimal familiarity with the "organizational culture" of a Parti Québécois government, would have persuaded the most skeptical of the fanaticism with which this government had made ready for its participation.

At no point was there any question of not taking part in the meetings or of actually boycotting them. Given that the items on the agenda were the very ones that had been given low priority by all Quebec governments, it would obviously be on rare occasions only that Quebec took the lead in suggesting compromises. Nor could there be any question of Quebec delegates trying to mediate the stands taken by other participants. It is a mistake, however, to think that all the Quebec government wanted was to see the talks end in failure, thus acquiring ammunition for its referendum. Quite the contrary: with any agreement, however trivial, the Quebec government could have promoted its qualities as a negotiator.

In the fall of 1978, only one Quebec cabinet minister had reservations (which were expressed privately to the premier) about Quebec's participation in the constitutional review process. By contrast, the majority position was that taking part, especially if it could produce an agreement, would give credence to the government's bargaining talents and would put more weight behind its aim of "seeking a mandate to negotiate" by means of a referendum. The arrival of the Clark government in Ottawa merely strengthened this belief.

The idea here is not to award points to the Parti Québécois government and praise its honesty, but to point out that it could hardly have behaved otherwise. It had every interest in seeing the talks succeed. As to whether it went along with the talks in the right way to make a contribution, or even whether its hopes for success could have been realistic in that context, this is an entirely different matter. As would also be noted, never did any of the participating governments deal directly with the issue of Quebec's place in the Canadian federation. All the Quebec government's efforts in this direction failed miserably. Nevertheless, it must not be thought that this concern with the conduct of the constitutional negotiations necessarily involved a critical view of the process as a whole.

No special attention was given to preparing for the post-referendum period. No "think tank" was set up for this purpose, except for two informal meetings among a few people, who included the deputy minister of intergovernmental affairs, the constitutional adviser to the premier and a judicial adviser. If the "yes" forces had won the referendum, everything would have had to be improvised.

Especially noted have been the organizational reasons for this absence of strategic planning. Mention must also be made of the belief that the referendum would only be one step in a long-drawn-out process. In fact, victory in the referendum was seen essentially as a means of getting English Canada to the negotiating table and freeing it from the federal government's tutelage. As proof of this, there was the unofficial "decision" of the aforementioned committee to recommend that the premier should not call a Quebec-Canada conference to formalize the process leading up to sovereignty association, but that he should present and explain the Quebec position in a more informal setting, namely at the conference of the eastern Canadian premiers and the governors of the New England states, and at the interprovincial conference which met every summer.

All the Canadian delegations were perfectly well aware of the approach favoured by the Quebec government in the event that the "yes" forces won the referendum. The Government of Ontario had even received several official and unofficial communications on this subject through its constitutional advisory committee.

The PQ government's reaction to the referendum defeat was just as quick and improvised. Within a few days, a brief memorandum to the executive council was produced and was approved by the cabinet without discussion. No attempt was made to analyze the causes of the loss. Rather, it was decided to plunge straight into the exercise called by the federal justice minister. There were two sets of reasons for this. One concerned votes, for a government refusal to negotiate in good faith would be perceived very negatively by the public and would turn the next election into a referendum poll. The other arose from the desire to salvage as much as possible and to prevent any constitutional change that would leave Quebec in a vulnerable position.

The Last Negotiation

In retrospect, the decision to take a full part in the post-referendum round of constitutional negotiations seems an eminently valid one. The immediate resignation of the government, to be succeeded in office by a Liberal party led by Claude Ryan, would have produced exactly the same results, since the form of political equality advocated in his party's beige paper was as unacceptable to other Canadian governments, federal and provincial, as sovereignty association was. With the Parti Québécois in opposition, demoralized and open to internal strife, Ryan's party would have had no striking force with which to negotiate anything that would be more or less acceptable to Quebec. We delude ourselves about the balance of power in Canadian Confederation if we imagine that any agreement is possible without the consent of the federal government. Moreover, the lack of official channels between the Liberal parties of Canada and Quebec, together with the animosity that arose between them in the referendum campaign, meant that disputes could not be dealt with informally.

The signing, together with seven other provinces, of an agreement that provided a basis of settlement for all parties, including Quebec, was not in itself really a tactical error. Voter considerations were not absent, of course, but these are unavoidable in any bargaining between governments. The fateful consequences of improvisation were not seen until later. Negotiated in the midst of the election campaign of April 1981, the entente lost much of its urgency with the victory of the Parti Québécois. The Quebec government's decision to ratify the agreement of "the eight," which was announced a few days later, must have surprised a good many of its sponsors.

At the time, the Quebec government saw this agreement not as a mere manoeuvre to put off a unilateral decision by Ottawa but as a genuine compromise on basics. In fact, this belief in its substance was the reason why the agreement was not rejected after the April election success. "If it was a good compromise in March, it is still a good compromise in May" seems to have been the thinking of the Government of Quebec. The error of judgment, then, lay not so much in the signing of the agreement as in an inability to recognize that the situation had just changed completely with the Parti Québécois' strong resurgence at the polls.

Throughout the summer of 1981, Quebec took part in the constitutional discussions, not only in good faith but with furious energy. In the end, it was this activity on Quebec's part, coupled with its partners' conviction that a rerun of Victoria was on the way, that caused the November debacle. Meeting individually with other provinces, the federal justice minister was at pains to stress the probable deceitfulness of Quebec, offering as proof the new activism and renewed political legitimacy of the PQ government.

This view of things was contrary in every respect to the post facto rationalization that kept going the rounds to the effect that the Parti Québécois would never have signed a constitutional agreement of any description with its Canadian partners. The facts said otherwise. In the first place, let it be pointed out that Quebec, along with seven other provinces, did indeed sign this agreement, the first such gesture by a

Quebec government since the constitutional "debate" had begun. Quebec's compromise on the amending formula and veto power is proof of the seriousness with which it was treating the whole matter.

Behind this argument lurked a view of Quebec and its government which one hesitates to describe. By definition, a Quebec government that asked for constitutional change was seen as somehow illegitimate, since by doing so it voted itself out of the club. Here was a flagrant example of how two political cultures had very different visions of the integrity of Canada's political concordat. For the English-Canadian negotiators, the "Us-Them" vision, which was so widespread in Quebec, had no meaning at all. They were unable to place themselves, conceptually or politically, outside the Canadian "we." Consequently, it was unacceptable to negotiate with Quebec on such a basis. This inability has never been understood in Quebec.

Probably because they were used to constitutional conferences, observers failed to see that the November 1981 meeting could not follow the pattern of its predecessors. On the surface, nothing looks more like a last-ditch conference than another last-ditch conference. All the ingredients of constitutional folklore were present: an interprovincial common front, rumours of dissension in this front, leaks of highly confidential strategic material, cynicism, hope.

Today, we have a better idea of just how much an acceptable agreement at the 1981 conference would have done for the Parti Québécois government. Of all the participants, it was probably the one with the most to gain (and so, inevitably, with the most to lose) from such an agreement. To realize this, all one has to do is take note of how the PQ lost ground after the fall of 1981. No fewer than six of its ministers resigned. The resignations snowballed. Dissension surfaced, and the party never again rose above the 30-percent mark in public support. The state of disaffection toward everything to do with the "national question," the lack of interest in all the federal-provincial squabbles blamed on the sterility of the government, and the substantial drop in support for sovereignty association were all symptoms that worsened after 1981. The arrival in Ottawa of Brian Mulroney's Conservative government and the pleasant thaw in Quebec-Ottawa relations that followed were accompanied at once by a slight Parti Québécois recovery in the polls. This confirmed that a climate of cordiality did no harm to the party's electoral chances, and in fact aided it; and unless we suppose that the Parti Québécois delighted in low popularity, we can assume that in 1981, as in 1984, a constitutional agreement with the central government would have suited it very well. It is a simple matter of strategic arithmetic, which goes badly with a conspiracy theory.

The Quebec government reached much the same conclusion in 1981 as in 1978: a satisfactory agreement with the rest of Canada would do more good than harm to the Government of Quebec, to Quebec society in general, and to the Parti Québécois in particular. The desire to reach agreement even prompted Quebec to suggest a preamble for the new Canadian Constitution, a preamble that was rejected by the other Canadian governments. It read as follows:

In accordance with the wishes of Canadians, the provinces of Canada, in concert with the federal government, choose to remain freely united in a federation as a sovereign and independent country under the Crown of Canada with a Constitution similar in its principles to that which Canada has known until now.

The basic goal of the federation is to preserve and promote freedom, justice and the well-being of all Canadians, which is to say:

to protect individual and collective rights, including those of aboriginal peoples;

to ensure that the laws and political institutions are founded on the will and consent of the people;

to promote the economic aspirations as well as the security and development of the various cultural groups of Canada;

to recognize the distinct character of the Quebec people which, with its francophone majority, forms one of the foundations of the Canadian duality; and

to contribute to the freedom and well-being of all humanity. [translation]

It is difficult to understand why the other Canadian governments felt called upon to reject this preamble. Of course, it came from a government which they were pleased to see as nothing less than an enemy. There was nothing in this view, however, to prevent the adoption of this declaration or a comparable declaration concerning the nature of Canadian society. This is the question that I shall deal with next.

Chapter 4

So Where Did English Canada Go?

English Canada's refusal, first to understand and then to accept the legitimate claims of Quebec is unquestionably one of the most firmly entrenched ideas of the Québécois elites. So much so, in fact, that we can speak in this case of an overall conviction that transcends party opinions, generation gaps, and political cultures. There are differences of opinion, of course, as to the reasons for this state of affairs and how it can be changed, but its reality cannot be called in doubt.

The beige paper produced by the Liberal party on the reform of federalism and the government's white paper on sovereignty association were in fact lengthy appeals for English Canada to rearrange its relationship with Quebec on a basis of greater equality. It is readily conceded that the appeals went unheard, but there was hope in both instances of making English Canada listen to reason either within the federal context or outside it. The refusal to respond confirmed certain images of the collective personality and interests of this English Canada.

Like its predecessors, this chapter makes no claim to the rewriting of history. Rather, the point is to put back into context some of the calm assertions about English Canada that are current in Quebec, dusting them off a little. It is pointless to stipulate that the interpretation offered here is that of a francophone Québécois. I am not setting out to establish a social profile of English Canada, however, but to try and explain why this English Canada has always refused to behave as one of the country's founding nations, a fact that of itself makes any political plan of equality between the two Canadian societies an impossibility.

But what connection does this have with everything that has just been said about Quebec's role in the constitutional negotiations? The answer this chapter hopes to give is this: Quebec's inability to bring a single, unified position to the conference table can be understood only in terms of the inability of English Canada to contemplate its own existence as a national collectivity. In two later chapters, I shall be examining the foreseeable consequences of this situation of mutual dependence, as well as the means of breaking the vicious circle.

It's All Durham's Fault

As will soon become obvious, our story, once more, goes back a long way. It was Lord Durham, sent over by London to inquire into "the Canadian political union and constitutional prospects," who became the first to recognize officially the existence of two nationalities in Canada. His diagnosis has gone down in history: "I expected to find a conflict between a government and a people: I found two nations warring in the bosom of a single state: I found a struggle, not of principles, but of races" (Durham, 1912 edn., vol. 2, p. 16). At a time of preparation to celebrate the 150th anniversary of these events, discussion of their real nature continues. Jean-Paul Bernard (1983) has reminded us recently that the story cannot be understood without a broad reading that takes in its national, social, and political dimension. Studying the historiographic production about the Rebellions of 1837–38, one is surprised to find the same grey areas, the same a priori statements, and the same absolutist conclusions as in the current debate — as if, in repeating itself, history has reproduced its own confusions as well.

The Durham Report's shrewdness came from the astonishing ease with which its author saw beyond (and sometimes flatly across) certain statements of intent from the protagonists. Of the French-Canadians, he said:

> [They] attempted to shroud their hostility to the influence of English immigration, and the introduction of British Institutions, under the guise of warfare against the government . . . [They invoked] the principles of popular control and democracy, and appealed with no little effort to the sympathy of liberal politicians in every quarter of the world (Durham, 1912 edn., vol. 2, p. 21 and 22).

What rubbish, said Durham. What the Canadians did not like was the English, not necessarily all English but certainly the ones who had settled among them and who wanted, not unnaturally, to fashion the economic, political, and social environment after their own image.

As for the English, Durham wrote that "finding their opponents in collision with the government, [they] have raised the cry of loyalty and attachment to the British connection." He hastened to add that the British authorities should not be fooled by these lamentations: what the English minority wanted was nothing more nor less than the elimination of the *Canadiens*, or at the very least "the protection of the prerogatives, which enable the few to resist the will of the many" (Durham, 1912 edn., vol. 2, p. 22). After this verdict, which at least had the virtue of frankness, its author was left with only two possible recommendations: permanent separation of the two nationalities, or removal of the very basis of the duality that made it impossible for any central government to function harmoniously. He would choose the latter, but not without stressing that there could not be a genuine middle road between the two.

The famous report's progress in the collective imagination of the two groups is proof of the accuracy of Durham's observations. It has a bad press today, but this is due essentially to a general refusal to be associated with certain of its author's unfortunate expressions. Yet Arthur Lower (1964, p. 251–53) refers to it as a penetrating analysis, one of the great documents of modern Liberalism, "one of the foundation stones of the modern English-speaking world."

In Quebec, careful note has been taken of the solution Durham suggested, as well as of some of his assertions about French-Canadian history and culture, but there has always been a refusal to give serious thought to the possibility that his report may actually have been Canada's political Magna Carta. It has often been cited as evidence — did we need more? — of the double-dealing and evil intent of the British newcomers, but there is something forced about this indignation, just as there is in other examples that are trotted out at opportune times: Riel, the Manitoba Schools Question, Regulation 17, conscription, and so on.

The picture Lord Durham gave of the French-Canadians led to a whole series of stereotypes, which still have a place of honour in the imagination of a good number of English-Canadians and which even get around in Quebec: a charming, joyous folk, little given to education or the economy, emotional and drawn to the things of the spirit. Each year still sees a few books and doctoral theses to prove that the Québécois lack the capitalist ethic of the anglophone "managers," and one has lost count of the articles pointing out how infatuated with business the younger generations are.

For Durham, the greatest service one could render these French-Canadians would be to put them in the way of the benefits of British civilization. Their situation was so sad and they were such realistic people, he wrote, that if the appropriate political framework was put in place they would cautiously assimilate. All that was needed was to alter the rules of the political game a little, and the logical process would do its work.

It is not really good form to bring up the Durham Report nowadays. In the reaction, one sees the vindictive spirit of a lagging nationalism. Things have changed indeed. The old battles, especially the old defeats, no longer have a place in a world of fresh challenges and computers. Nonetheless. . . .

To see Durham's plan as a coldly reasoned venture in cultural and political genocide would mean falling prey to a paranoid view of history. Durham himself was too familiar with the Irish Question to believe for one moment that such a solution had any chance of working in Canada. He had resigned from the British cabinet over the passage of the Coercion Bill. We should therefore not refer to the Durham Report as a plan of action or even as a policy which later became the behaviour pattern for English Canada's political elites. Such teleological visions of history cannot stand up to the march of events. Still, we should not be too quick to conclude that Durham's analysis was unrelated to reality.

French-Canadian historiography has missed the essence of the celebrated report. What Durham advised the English of Canada to do was not to attack the *Canadiens* but to stop behaving as a minority — which they were, statistically, at the time — and to turn themselves into the political and economic majority of the country. The linguistic and demographic majorities would follow inevitably. In short, what Durham recommended was that the English should create the Canadian nation and take possession of it. To achieve this, the judicial and political foundations of the new nation had to be laid down. National feeling could then develop naturally.

This inclination for settling ethnic and national imbroglios politically was nothing new with Durham. He had already suggested the same solution for Belgium, Ireland, Poland, and the Rhineland. The Canadian example never struck him as insuperable or much different from similar situations encountered in Europe.

Durham regarded with impatience and contempt the many squabbles that divided the English of Canada: Anglicans versus Presbyterians, Catholics versus Protestants, the Family Compact versus the Château Clique, merchants versus gentlemen farmers. Such squabbling was simply a waste of time, he thought, and was holding back the development of the country. It would be better to leave these parish feuds exclusively to the French-Canadians. His attitude to the latter, if one takes the trouble to read attentively, was one of benign neglect: treat them with respect as far as their religion goes, but douse them with indifference by incorporating them into a single political structure, and then let time do its work. . . . Without in the least suspecting it, Durham may already have understood that religion would soon lose prominence to political institutions, especially if these were to become representative institutions.

It has long been believed in Quebec (and this was always the case with a strong majority of the political elite) that English Canada was built "against" French Canada. This does us great honour, but it does not at all correspond to reality, nor was this what Durham and those who came after him had in mind. If there was in fact an inner logic to their actions, it reflected a process in which French Canada (and this goes even more for Quebec) has always been relatively absent, except at those times when it has managed to assert itself and impose its own agenda. For English

Canada — and I shall continue to call it this for the time being — Quebec as a distinct political and national collectivity has never been more than one contributing element in the business of building the country. From an English-Canadian point of view, then, the accusations of basic, permanent historical opposition between the two societies are without meaning, and there can therefore be no thought of responding to them or remedying them.

Since Durham, it has been clear that those familiarly known as English-Canadians have never been interested in building English Canada. Their only such frame of reference has been an undifferentiated Canada. As a result, their energies have never been directed against the French-Canadians, except when the latter have tried to impose a political duality which they do not accept as legitimate. In this sense, they are not and never have been *against* Quebec. They are *for* Canada.

Paradoxically, the historians and elites of the two groups have not absorbed the same aspects of the Durham Report. In the one group, they have been impressed above all by the suggested solution, the creation of a single nation-state. In the other, the choice has been to remember the diagnosis: the existence of two national collectivities.

Durham had no fondness for the *Canadiens*, but at least he acknowledged their existence as a distinct national group. By implication, without dwelling too much on this, he assigned an identical status to the British element. At that time even more than today, talk of English Canada belonged to the world of imagination. Upper Canada, that problematic collection of individuals, had been in existence barely 50 years. The majority of its residents had not been born in North America, and the ties with Britain still took pride of place. Durham himself realized this when he wrote that it was "much more difficult to form an accurate idea of the state of Upper than of Lower Canada" (Durham, 1969 edn., p. 59). In the end, he spent only two days in Toronto and took full advantage of his stay there to visit Niagara Falls. As for the Atlantic colonies, their relations with Canada were extremely tenuous, and Durham merely pointed out that in that region "all are united and zealous on the capital point of the maintenance of the tie with Great Britain" (Durham, 1969 edn., p. 83).

There is an element of irony in a report that acknowledged both the existence of a French-Canadian nation and the need to restrict its manoeuvring room as far as possible by a judicious combination of institutional enclosure and demographic repression. A strange recognition indeed.

In this respect, the current reality of the approach taken by John George Lambton, Earl of Durham, cannot be doubted. English Canada frequently recognizes the equality of Quebec when it is a question of defining the Canadian problem, only to deny it when the time comes to consider solutions for this Canadian sickness. Equal in terms of the problem but not equal in terms of the solution — this seems to have emerged as a constant in the political thinking of English Canada when it has to define itself in relation to Quebec.

The continuity is striking between the English-Canadian fragment and political culture as it was defined in mid-19th-century England. One finds in Durham, and after him in many "definers of situations" in English Canada, a strain of liberalism that mingles condescension with calculation. This is the liberalism of the dominant, of the man who accepts no challenge to his motives or to his solution. This brand of liberalism, forever seeking good causes to defend, makes one think of those British engineers who at this same time, from Calcutta to Valparaiso, were forever seeking new rail lines to build. But that is another story.

The Durham Connection

The English-Canadian community has always been divided on a host of issues in debates that have never found more than very scattered echoes in Quebec: centralizers versus decentralizers, left versus right, nationalists versus anti-nationalists, Europeans versus Americans, laymen versus clergy. Yet any survey, however brief, of the intellectual history of English Canada since Durham should be enough to reveal:

- that none of these quarrels was ever about the type of political partnership to establish with Quebec, since Quebec as a distinct political society is not part of the English-Canadian universe of possibilities;
- that none of these quarrels was ever about English-Canadian identity or about the meaning to be given to that expression, since there has never been any question of a distinct political development for English Canada; and
- that there has never been any question, in the rest of Canada, of a thorough overhaul of the political definition of the country and its underlying nation-state. This definition — parliamentary, federal, and symmetrical — is an integral part of the very definition given of Canadian society.

These three statements, which obviously will have to be refined somewhat later on, do not mean that the elites and intellectuals of English Canada are unconcerned about the place of French-Canadians in the federative whole, or that they have asked themselves no questions about the country's cultural autonomy in relation to the United States. Always, however, the thinking has been about the place of the French-Canadians within the Canadian mosaic, not about a political partnership with Quebec; or, again, the questions have been about the Canadian identity, not about the meaning of the English-Canadian identity. English Canada as food for thought arouses even less enthusiasm in English Canada than it does in Quebec. This says it all. A bibliography of works on English Canada would have very few titles in it. Moreover, this dearth seems not to have been noticed and worries no one. English-Canadian commentators, so quick to disclose the smallest details about their economic or cultural dependence, are not unduly concerned about this lack of collective identity; for their identity exists at another level, at the level of Canada as a whole.

In more than 60 years of publication, the periodical *Canadian Forum* has never vouchsafed more than a few allusions to the theme of English Canada (Granatstein and Stevens, 1972). On occasion, studies with promising titles appear. This was the case with J.L. Elliott's collection, *Two Nations, Many Cultures* (1979). Curiously, however, the 30 articles in the book were grouped in three sections as follows; "Native People," "The Second Nation: The French in Canada," and "The Other Ethnic Groups: The Non-English in English Canada." The "first nation," then, is completely ignored, unless it is the defining of English Canada on the basis of those who are not of British origin! The "ethnic" studies, obviously the latest rage in the universities, never attribute ethnic group status to the English-Canadians, not even to those living in Quebec. On the other hand, they show loving concern for the Québécois and French-Canadians generally (Goldstein and Bienvenue, 1980; Dahlie and Fernando, 1981).

Also, an author will occassionally announce that although the reality of English Canada is not truly entrenched in the political reality of the country, the idea of this Canada is not altogether defunct and it ought to be encouraged. In 1965, for example, the sociologist Gad Horowitz became unquestionably the first and probably still the only person to suggest a binational approach to the Canadian situation:

> There should exist an English-Canadian nation, and not just a collection of provinces associated with a French-Canadian nation. . . . It is time to accept and recognize the demands of French Canada as legitimate by making the same demands for ourselves. These are perfectly normal demands. Enriching relationships are possible only between two people with a certain degree of maturity. The same goes for nations, whether they exist within a single state or not (Horowitz, 1965, p. 32; translation).

Appeals of this kind have been received at best with indifference and most of the time with marked hostility. When Horowitz (1966) advanced the hypothesis that the term *Toryism* defined the ideological heartland of English Canada's political culture and distinguished it from American liberalism, his suggestion stirred up a controversy that is still not ready to die down (Horowitz, 1978). Ever since the American sociologist S.M. Lipset (1970) dared to point out a conservative and elitist strain in English-Canadian culture, attempts of this type have grown rarer; so pervasive does the notion seem to have become that there is no English-Canadian nation, culture, collective personality or identity. The conclusion of A.B. Anderson and J.S. Frideres, which ends a survey of under two pages on the subject, is a good summary of the dominant point of view:

> The British-Canadians are too widespread geographically, too similar to Americans, too diversified in terms of religion, and above all too unsure of how much or how little to emphasize their heritage, to be a nation as the French-Canadians are (Anderson and Frideres, 1981, p. 84).

The irony here is too great and too touching to be ignored. English Canada, which by its own definition does not exist, is denying the other Canadian nation, whose existence it does not question, a form of political life that is consistent with its admitted reality. What a strange division of labour this is, between an English Canada which takes up all the political stage and a French Canada which is freely granted the whole stage of nationality! Can one imagine two peoples more comfortable in their mutual dependence?

In the political universe of English Canada, Quebec is often associated with a source of worry, of stress. Or else it is simply ignored in silence. Ever since 1960, Quebec has been looked on as a type of illness. This being the only collective recognition that the Québécois have ever received, they have accepted it with alacrity, even with a twinge of satisfaction. Yet this very special recognition has prompted Quebec's elites to hold the misconception that the "Quebec problem" has become an essential element in the "Canadian problem". The result of this has been a profound confusion, which has still not been cleared up.

For many members of the Quebec political elite, especially those of the post-1960 generation, the "Canadian connection" has always assumed a problematic character, or, more precisely, an interrogatory character. These people have always seen Canada as a question about Quebec's national identity; for them, English Canada is the mythic haunt of individuals whose favourite question is "What does Quebec want?"

If, in Quebec's case, the "Canadian question" is a basic fact of the political situation and even of its own national identity, English Canada's case is very different. The erruption of the "Quebec question" is a recent and really quite superficial phenomenon. Each of the three great political traditions that coexist in English Canada has developed its own view of the Quebec problem; of course, their sensibilities differ, but beyond these differences there is underlying unanimity. Until now, this unanimity has gone unnoticed in Quebec. Without it, however, the surprising finale of the constitutional review process cannot be understood. Any other explanation has to rely on a conspiracy theory which does not correspond with the facts.

Obviously, this outline will not reflect the full richness of English Canada's cultural traditions. In each area, I have chosen a few authors whom I see as representative and as particularly enlightening.

The Liberal Tradition

Canadian liberalism is too diverse for anyone to define its essence in a few pages. I shall therefore focus on the place that the nation, nationalism, and Quebec occupy in it.

Arguing the thesis that nationalism is the great enemy of liberalism and thus of progress and reason, Ramsay Cook has written:

> We have had too much nationalism, not too little in Canada. . . . But what value, it may be asked, is a nation-state without nationalism? Except for those with an unquenchable thirst for ideological certainty and national purity, the answer should be self-evident: . . . organizing groups of people into manageable units and providing them with services which they need and which they can share: a railway, an art gallery. . . . Not perhaps the heady stuff from which Garibaldis or Guevaras are made. But then, Canada is neither a nineteenth-century Italy nor a twentieth-century Cuba (Cook, 1971, p. 14).

The nation-state is an unfortunate necessity, making it possible to perform certain functional tasks. Overidentifying with the nation, however, is to be avoided at all costs. Here are the great themes of the classic anti-nationalist thesis. It is hard to tell how widespread it is in English Canada. Is it not the stuff of any hegemonic nationalism to define itself as universal and even nonexistent? In this respect, nationalism is like any other ideology. One recalls what Marx had to say about the so-called quest for universality of all ruling classes, which like to appear as defenders of common interests against sectarian particularism. This largely explains the discretion that surrounds English-Canadian nationalism, and even Canadian nationalism, in the universities of English Canada. No dominant nationalism cares to discuss itself, preferring to be moved by the nationalism of others. People were always surprised that Pierre Trudeau, who was said to be the ultimate anti-nationalist, would deign on occasion to use the nationalist argument. The surprise was perhaps not so much the judicious use in itself as the arresting ease with which it was done.

For Ramsay Cook, Quebec nationalism is barely acceptable when it accompanies the process of sociopolitical modernization. It becomes downright intolerable when it surfaces in some political scheme.

At times, this anti-nationalism comes out in a messianism that has few known equals anywhere. This other liberal tradition endlessly proclaims that Canada does not belong to itself, since the only reason for its existence is to stand guard for human civilization. This particular view has surfaced mainly in the foreign policy sector. In Quebec, it prompts a few smiles. In the words of John Holmes, however, it takes on a nobility which we would be wrong to ridicule:

> For Canada, unlike the heroic Nation-State of old, national survival is not

the highest priority of foreign policy. The survival of the world, or at least of our kind of civilization, comes first. There are many things more important for us than resisting our absorption . . . into an Atlantic state or even our national extinction through absorption by the United States. If either of these acts was essential to save ourselves and others from nuclear annihilation or totalitarian enslavement, we would undoubtedly accept them (Holmes, 1966, p. 218).

If nationalism cannot be made to disappear, it is essential for Canada to place its own version of it at the disposal of a higher interest, that of human civilization.

Is there any need to point out here that this approach leaves very little room for the Quebec question, which cannot but look frivolous beside the vastness and significance of the great work to be done? Moreover, this kind of ethnic problem harms Canada's image. It is hard to be the self-appointed conscience of the planet when a certain number of internal issues remain unresolved.

Canada's internationalists will not come out and admit this, but they have always been a little ashamed about the persistence of the "Quebec problem." In this they are joined by a good number from the Quebec elites, who often leave their "Quebecness" at the provincial border and prefer to go unnoticed in foreign parts. Nationalism gets a decidedly poor press even from those who profess it the most openly. For these liberal internationalists, it was the final straw when Quebec burst upon the world stage. The move could only be read as a challenge to the very basis of Canada's existence. No form of messianism, whether religious or internationalist, is tolerant of competition. One has seen so many English-Canadian liberals, who are ready with all manner of generosity when it is for Indonesia or Bangladesh, turn into carping legalists when the time comes to discuss Quebec.

The "Quebec question" is not altogether absent from these international concerns. It will at least have brought out the virtues of an external policy that reflects the bilingual and bicultural character of the country. This has automatically increased the area of international messianism's operations, and new myths and clichés have appeared, including one to the effect that "Canadians are well received in Africa because they have no colonialist past." It takes a very poor understanding of the basis of neo-colonialism and its importance for the local ruling elites to imagine that this is necessarily a big advantage. But that is another question, or rather, it is an example of the significant distortion which can be produced by translating poor perceptions of the Canadian political reality into foreign-policy terms. Between these two spheres, internal and external, there is much traffic and mutual reinforcement of myths and biases, and this inevitably creates great disfunction.

One thing is certain: there could be no question in this area of taking any French-Canadian opinion whatever into account. In any case, to the extent that such opinion exists, it simply strengthens the orientation that the internationalists want to give to Canadian foreign policy:

> It seems to me our own traditional middle-power policy is not incompatible with the French-Canadians' consensus on what our national foreign policy should be. . . . If anything, French-Canadians would propel us further in the direction we have been moving (Holmes, 1966, p. 216).

To be avoided at any price, however, is the double danger of a distinct foreign policy for Quebec, or even a Canadian foreign policy that comes from some sort of negotiation between the two levels of government. It is easy to understand why Holmes decides that this duality would inevitably work to Canada's disadvantage. Even if his is a rather simplistic view, it can still be defended in terms of coherence. The surprise in Holmes's argument comes in the explanation he offers before concluding that it would be dangerous for the Québécois themselves if they had their own international viewpoint:

> It is not in the national interest to create the machinery or encourage the assumptions which could lead to separate foreign policies. It is not in the interests of French Canada to do so, for the inevitable result would be to surrender the determination of federal foreign policy to the sole control of English-Canadians. An effective foreign policy cannot be evolved in a provincial capital because it is divorced from the international life of diplomacy, conferences, negotiations, secrets and confidences. French Canada is more likely to play a significant role in world affairs through a state of twenty millions than as an independent state of five million people (Holmes, 1966, p. 218).

Quite apart from the paternalism of these remarks, which is a little reminiscent of certain American attitudes toward Canadian pretensions to independence in foreign and economic policy, they tell us something about the extreme sensitivity that English-Canadian liberalism and internationalism have about the image that this country projects on the world scene. This sensitivity is simply the reflection of deep-rooted dependence. The makers of Quebec's external policy soon learned to use it for amusement in order to make their federal colleagues "climb the drapes." This contempt for English Canada's cultural, economic, and political dependence, so handy in terms of the psychological comfort it provides, has nonetheless warped Quebec's perceptions considerably.

The Tory Tradition, Red or Otherwise

There remains the Canadian nation, the one that stretches going from coast to coast. The place that English Canada assigns to the French-Canadian nation in this Canadian identity is not really an impressive one, for all the denials. From Hugh MacLennan and his two solitudes through George Grant and W.L. Morton, an entire generation of English-Canadian intellectuals produced pages of fine melancholy on the impossibility of isolating this Canadian identity. In his *Lament for a Nation* (1965) Grant could calmly announce Canada's demise without having to devote more than a few paragraphs to French Canada. Morton was more generous in *The Canadian Identity* (1972); the French fact is present from page 4 to 14, though it was expelled from the Canadian identity definitively in 1760. In the second edition, released in 1981, French Canada appears in a supplementary chapter, which is evocatively called "Canada Under Stress."

Whereas Ramsay Cook wanted Canada to become the first nation-state that did not need nationalist cement to hold it together, Donald Smiley would like Canadians to acquire a common political nationality without, however, falling into the trap of nationalism. On the whole, this viewpoint has gone completely unnoticed in Quebec, even though it recalls some of the traditional French-Canadian attitudes to the *Constitution Act, 1867*.

For Smiley, political communities could not be imagined without a relationship of special allegiance linking citizen and community. On this point, we get the complete reverse of the liberal anti-nationalist position:

> It seems likely that a politically organized society cannot in the long run survive without the capacity to appeal effectively to the will and imagination of its citizens, particularly one so little formed as that of Canada and so vulnerable to disintegrative forces from within and assimilative pressures from without (Smiley, 1967, p. 129).

Yet this allegiance must not have a sentimental or irrational basis which would point it fatally towards totalitarian attitudes and practices. It must be primarily political, which actually corresponds to Canadian political tradition:

> Canada was from the first and continues to be . . . a community of political allegiance alone. The Confederation settlement was deliberately designed to make the claims of citizenship in the new Dominion compatible with other loyalties (Smiley, 1967, p. 130).

When it comes right down to it, Smiley opposes any collective identification of those individuals who could come to break their allegiance to the Canadian political system:

> We have had too much of racial nationalism — of French-Canadian delusions of a providential mission, of notions of British Imperial Destiny, of latter-day Anglo-Saxon assimilationism. These deviations . . . have been destructive both of human values and of the Canadian Confederation. . . . French-Canadians are now articulating their demands in other than the older racial-religious terms (Smiley, 1967, p. 130).

Smiley's communalism, however, leaves the Quebec fact no more room than earlier writers did with their appeals to reason and progress, or to universality. What concerns Smiley is the relationship between the citizens and the state, especially when this state has the pretension to define the common good and the means of making sure that its definition is applied. It is in the light of this problem, namely that of the modern Leviathan, that Smiley views the whole issue of Quebec-Canada relations. Any attempt to give political existence to Canada's cultural duality will be rejected automatically as a threat to the community-type relations which must join all Canadians together. Any institutional solution will be rejected automatically because it would irrevocably lead to growth in the influence of the state and of those who speak in its name. Smiley's refusal is total and spares none of the options put forward as alternatives to Quebec sovereignty:

- *Special Status*
  Despite its logical attractiveness, the almost inevitable result of implementing the "statut particulier" would be the separation of Quebec through attrition (Smiley, 1967, p. 106).
- *Cooperative Federalism*
  The ongoing process of cooperative federalism results both in ineffective government and in the continuing attenuation of the power of the federal authorities (Smiley, 1967, p. 103).
- *Binationalism*
  The definition of equal partnership between English- and French-Canadians in terms of collectivities leads directly to the establishment of a fully independent Quebec (Smiley, 1967, p. 116).
- *Interprovincial Pact*
  The passing of the two-nations debate appears to be leading to a new orthodoxy that Canada is no nation at all but rather a loose union of provinces. . . . This [special status for all] may result in the destruction of Canada. . . if Quebec by such procedures and with the consent of a majority of its people, negotiates its way out (Smiley, 1976, p. 225 and 226).
- *New Constitution*
  In the present period of conflict . . . it seems improbable. . . . Furthermore, a preoccupation with explicit constitutional reform may both divert Canadians from attainable solutions to more pressing matters and attenuate further the legitimacy of the existing Constitution without replacing it (Smiley, 1967, p. 105).
- *Full Respect for the Constitutional Act, 1867*
  The alternative of returning to the situation which in its essential aspects existed before the First World War is, I believe, impractical. There has grown up a tradition of federal involvement in many important matters within provincial legislative jurisdiction (Smiley, 1967, p. 105 and 106).

By definition, this insistence on the political collectivity as the basis of

Canadian identity leaves no room for competition by a Quebec political collectivity that would ask the same allegiance of its citizens. The similarity here with some frequently expressed concerns of Sir John A. Macdonald is not mere coincidence. In both cases, there is the intention to create a new nationality which, failing the eradication of geographical, ethnic and religious elements, would still transcend these through a deeper allegiance.

In Quebec, there has been a tendency to associate this approach with a cast of mind that is reactionary, anti-French, anti-Quebec, traditionalist, and so on. Here is another error of judgment. Disregarding for a moment the Canadian context in which this view was necessarily developed and looking only at its substance, we find a definition of the political collectivity that is not in the least reactionary. For Smiley, this collectivity is nothing more than the pooling of the mutual requirements that individuals and groups have of themselves and of others. The political structure is present simply to honour these requirements and to place collective decisions at the service of the people's welfare.

Of these mutual requirements, Smiley mentions ten which command a broad consensus, both on the right and on the left, and in English Canada as well as in Quebec:

- equality before the law;
- a generous and effective social welfare system;
- the eradication of regional economic disparities;
- an equitable sharing of fiscal resources;
- a dynamic culture;
- the sharing of energy resources;
- access to government services in the language of the citizens;
- consideration of the claims of aboriginal peoples;
- the necessity for government policies to be adapted to the needs of the citizens, and not the reverse; and
- a foreign policy based on peace and development.

That such a program should not have a word to say about rebuilding the country so as to entrench recognition of the political equality of Quebec and French Canada again shows the inability to see Quebec as a different component in the Canadian enterprise. In this sense, Donald Smiley has furnished us with eloquent proof that in English Canada the spaciousness of a political vision in no way depends on the role played in it by Quebec. It is easier now to see how so open a mind could find it completely impossible to understand (and still less to accept) anything at all in Gérard Bergeron's thesis on the need to change the Canadian federation into a super-Commonwealth of two and ten. There followed the familiar debate between these two men, one of whom, quite obviously and in the greatest good faith, had not the faintest idea of the logic of the remarks of the other.

Like the liberals and the internationalists, Quebec is stuck at the outer edge of Canada's political universe. It is, of course, an important element in that universe, so important that it is hard to imagine a Canada without it, but its very importance ensures that the delicate balance of the Canadian equation cannot be touched in its entirety.

Meanwhile, on the Left

Here again, the streams of thought that define what is generally known as the English-Canadian progressive tradition are so numerous that one hesitates to make the count: agrarian radicalism, the Social Gospel, the New Left, the Waffle, the CCF, the New Democrats, the League for Social Reconstruction, and the radicals. All of them build and decline as dictated by defeat at the polls, by American imports, or by the concerns of the time, to the point where one could get the impression that everything always has to begin all over again.

For a while, between 1965 and 1970, Quebec held an important place in debates among these factions. However, after the defeat that Pierre Trudeau administered to the "two nations" theory in the 1968 election, and particularly with the electoral rise of the Parti Québécois, Quebec was relegated to the sidelines once more. Taken overall, these English-Canadian progressives' position on Quebec turned on an axis running from feelings of annoyance to a kind of deluded paternalism.

The classic view of the English-Canadian Communists was summed up succinctly by Tim Buck, the founder of the Communist Party of Canada, in some short-form notes he made for a 1926 speech: "French Canadians: Not to be exaggerated. Anti-British tendencies, also chauvinistic tendencies." Today, this paternalistic attitude still governs the viewpoint of the Canadian Communist left. Quebec's nationalism and independentism are not forgiven for their supposedly *petit bourgeois* origins. This thinking is current far beyond the very limited circles of Canada's Communist movement. It has been subscribed to by the entire Canadian left.

Garth Stevenson's position is one of the most developed. For him, the whole separatist movement is merely a sublimation of the class conflicts that are tearing at Quebec society and enabling a new lower-middle class to build its power. The movement is made more dangerous by the fact that if ever this class managed to succeed in its project, Quebec might well be facing state totalitarianism, a swing to the right, and American domination. In short, it would be the Apocalypse. Nothing could therefore be more natural than to conclude:

> Measured against such a project, even the frustrations of the status quo must appear at least relatively appealing to all but the minority of committed separatists (Stevenson, 1979, p. 274).

Moreover, an independent Quebec, a real banana republic, would inevitably whet the appetite of the Americans for a move into the rest of Canada. Probably, though, they would not take the trouble to intervene actively in Quebec, since the Québécois republic would have no alternative except to settle as best it could under U.S. hegemony (Stevenson, 1979, p. 97).

Stevenson's points are simply reworkings of the old centralizing theses of the CCF and NDP. They are often compared with the approach, presumed to be more constructive, of the English-Canadian New Left. Such is not the case, however. The New Left offers no outright support for the political equality of the two national collectivities. In fact, with a few exceptions, the very existence of English Canada gets little more recognition than it does in writings from the other intellectual traditions. As far as the "Quebec problem" goes, this group's concerns are support for Quebec's right to self-determination and a refusal to contemplate the use of force. Much is made of this position in the English-Canadian left, though it looks exactly like a position that has been expressed on many occasions by Pierre Trudeau.

This recognition marks the high point of the sympathy that is shown for Quebec's independentist arguments by the left of English Canada. Oddly enough, during the entire referendum campaign of 1980 not one single English-Canadian left-wing group came out in support of the "yes" thesis, which called for direct negotiation based on the proposals for Quebec sovereignty. I shall not pause here to discuss the pertinence or substance of the sovereignty theses. I must observe, however, that they did not arouse any real sympathy in these left-wing groups, who might have been expected to emerge as natural allies.

For obvious tactical reasons, Quebec's independentist elites have always chosen to ignore this unexpected lack of support in English Canada. Their decision has been simply to emphasize the support that would be generated around the issue of the right to self-determination. These tactical manoeuvres, however, have obscured the basic fact, which is the inability of the English-Canadian progressive movements to absorb the possibility of a major overhaul of the Canadian system, not to mention that of a sovereign political society in Quebec. When it comes down to a realistic estimate of support for their views in English Canada, Quebec's independentists, in their short-sightedness, are not unlike the Quebec supporters of renewed federalism.

It will be argued that the English-Canadian left could not go beyond its support for Quebec's right to self-determination for fear of being labelled interventionist. There is not the same caution, however, when it is a matter of support for all sorts of different causes, just so long as they do not involve an immediate neighbour. In many cases, the solidarity for self-determination came coupled with numerous warnings about the genuinely democratic nature of this type of consultation. It seems that the very idea of a referendum on the political organization best suited to the country received very little support in English Canada. There is not the trace of a proposal concerning the need to have such a consultation.

With the constitutional conference of 1981 and the agreement that came out of it, the unimportance of the binational vision of the country in the eyes of English Canada's progressives could be highlighted even more clearly. All they did was express regret that Quebec, for reasons which they scrupulously avoided describing as valid, had not thought it best to accept an agreement which was "certainly not perfect but was real nonetheless." Their reservations about the constitutional agreement had more connection with lacunae in the area of personal freedoms than with the absence of recognition of the country's binational reality.

Rejecting the anti-nationalism of some liberals, the English-Canadian left embraced the cause of Canadian nationalism without reservation, not realizing that Canadian nationalism was essentially an English-Canadian nationalism, which was unaware of its own existence. These nationalists, only yesterday the merciless critics of Liberal party policy, climbed over one another to declare support for any Trudeau government measure, so long as it was wrapped in a pro-Canada speech. So it was that Mel Watkins, one of the founders of the Waffle, and Walter Gordon and Mel Hurtig, two co-founders of the Committee for an Independent Canada, along with Abe Rotstein, the dean of economic nationalism, became the enthusiastic champions of the National Energy Policy.

Reading their latest writings, one senses relief at not having to discuss the "Quebec problem" any more: they do not realize that there can be no genuine solution to the Canadian question without a satisfactory answer to the Quebec question (Watkins, 1981; Rotstein, 1981). Periodicals like *Canadian Forum*, *Canadian Dimension* and *This Magazine* took positions that were full of inconsistencies, supporting editorially what was gainsaid in individual articles, or vice versa.

Donald Smiley has pointed out the extreme decay that had overtaken Canadian nationalism, or at least its so-called progressive variety:

The reconciliation between P.E. Trudeau and major elements of the nationalist intelligentsia of English-speaking Canada is one of the more unusual mini-themes of Canadian politics. . . . It is not clear why and how R. Lévesque and the PQ were jettisoned by the nationalist illuminati of English-speaking Canada. Prior to the referendum these people regarded Lévesque as the best thing . . . since sliced bread. . . . There is no new Trudeau, there is a remarkable consistency between the attitudes and actions of the Trudeau of "Octobre 1970" and the Trudeau of 1980, a ruthless impulse to mobilize whatever instruments are available to him to impose his will and his vision of Canada (Smiley, 1980, pp. 20–21).

The Specialists

The division of English Canada's political culture into three great families had no other purpose than to prove that none of these traditions had any place to speak of for Quebec, and even less for a binational vision of the country. These pages may have given the impression that very few English-Canadian intellectuals had given consideration to the interwoven themes of the relations between the federal and provincial governments, between English Canada and French Canada, and between Quebec and Canada. This obviously does not correspond to reality. In English Canada, as in Quebec, a distinct intellectual community sprang up which turned these questions into a genuine industry. This is the group that I shall now examine, though realizing that the collection is somewhat artificial in view of the significant differences of opinion among the leading protagonists. In spite of these differences, however, a common image of Quebec emerges with enough clarity to be worthy of the name.

Another group, which could affectionately be called the Quebec Watchers or the School of Queen's (the Gang of Four, the Kingston Trio!), showed a more receptive attitude to Quebec and Quebec's claims. In contrast to Donald Smiley, their definition of the Canadian political space hinged to some extent on the problem of Quebec.

For Quebec had emerged as a problem, a challenge to Canadian ingenuity. There was a frequent tendency to play with catastrophe — "to think about the unthinkable," Herman Kahn would have said — to think about the possibility that Quebec would finally achieve the status of a sovereign state and would put paid to the Canada of ten provinces. This flirtation with the unthinkable was enlightening about some realities with which the Québécois were largely unfamiliar, especially the permanence of the federal system even in the event of Quebec's withdrawal, since it was the only system that could accommodate the regional characteristics. One surprising thing (or was it really?) was that none of these scenarios of the unthinkable took into account the great upheaval Quebec's departure would cause in the modus operandi of the Canadian political system. The very omission of this element confirms how little Quebec's national reality had been integrated into the operation of this system.

These games with the unthinkable also distorted the perceptions of Quebec's political elites, the supporters of sovereignty as well as those of a remodelled federalism. They cemented their conviction that public opinion and an intelligentsia did indeed exist in English Canada and that this latter group, when the time came, would agree to a discussion between equals about either binational federalism or sovereignty association. By thinking the unthinkable, the Quebec Watchers had unwittingly reinforced the impression that there was a desire to negotiate, since there was also a plan that gave a rational basis to such a desire. In fact, the impression was only an illusion: it fell to pieces with the constitutional coup of 1981. What the Québécois took as indicating a desire to rebuild political relations between the two collectivities was actually nothing but a resigned acceptance of the idea of Quebec's withdrawal.

In that group's many analyses, Quebec was perceived above all as a culture, not as a political society. What they appreciated in Quebec was the "difference" it imposed on Canada. They chose to make this language difference part of the Canadian identity rather than acknowledging that it had meaning and value only when it was integrated into the political, cultural, and economic systems. Here, we are in the presence of another of the many facets of the Canadian paradox. English Canada, which does not exist, or at least which is bent on proclaiming its nonexistence, needs its antithesis to demonstrate that the Canadian reality is "different." In short, the French-Canadian or francophone minority allows English Canada to dispense with the search for its own identity.

This "difference" imposed by the presence of French-Canadians demands nonetheless that they continue in their minority role. In Quebec, there was never a proper assessment — at least in the version put forward by the English-Canadians — of the implications, for Canadian identiy, of Quebec's desire to be dealt with as a distinct political entity. Without the French-Canadian minority, English Canada's claim to its own difference from the United States would be considerably threatened.

Quebec was seen, then, as the special place of a language and possibly a culture that should be protected. Thus, the introduction to *Le Canada face à son destin* declared stoutly: "We recognize that Quebec needs autonomy and assurance of the survival of its culture." This recognition was not disinterested, however, since "for each of us, Canada's promising future, the unique character of the country, flow from the bilingual and pluricultural nature of its society" (Simeon, 1978, p. 4). It will have been noted that this right to be different was essentially associated with the duality of languages, and also with the country's multicultural profile. Here we can see precisely how the vision of Canada promoted by Pierre Trudeau, a vision opposed in every detail to that put forward by André Laurendeau and the first team of the Royal Commission on Bilingualism and Biculturalism, had penetrated even to the most francophile of English-Canadian observers.

Although the greatest admiration was shown for Quebec culture, the same did not apply when it came to the political maturity of the Québécois and their capacity to organize their own political area. To what extent did this pessimism reflect a similar pessimism about English-Canadian culture? John Meisel, one of the most influential and respected members of this group, used some surprising terms to register his concern for the future of a sovereign political society in Quebec:

> The third factor that prompts doubt that Quebec can better reach its objectives by separating from Canada has to do with the fragility of all democratic systems. Democratic institutions can, alas, degenerate easily into totalitarian regimes. . . . Quebec is undergoing so rapid, so radical a transformation . . . all this could prevent the present regime from stopping development towards a regimented system, destructive of freedoms (Meisel, 1978, p. 346; translation).

One is left more or less speechless by this thesis, especially coming from one of the English-Canadians who has best understood the aspirations of Quebec.

The dangers evoked by John Meisel are real, but they are not inherent in all political societies or in all use of power. The cultural influence of the United States, its economic hegemony, and its political heft are dangers that are just as threatening to all non-U.S. political societies in this hemisphere. This is the price we have to pay for being North Americans. These dangers exist even for Canada and English Canada, except that in their case the point of no return has already been reached and, by this very fact, the danger does not exist any more (unfortunately).

One of the most curious aspects of the attitude of this group is the variety of its reactions to the independentist program and its formula for sovereignty association. They will acknowledge that the idea of independence is legitimate, attractive, legal, and probably achievable. They are ready to believe that it is shared by the most dynamic and progressive elements in Quebec's population: artists, union activists, journalists, teachers, scientists, feminists. However, all this support and the obvious respect with which they greet the independentist option does not prevent them from opposing it. This attitude is in remarkable contrast to the contempt they heap on the sovereignty association model. They charge it with being simply a way for the Québécois to have their cake and eat it. This amounts to saying that the sovereignty-association supporters are at best poor in spirit for suggesting their formula and at worst a bunch of upstarts, devoid of all sense of fairness.

The taste for having one's cake at any price is the essence of politics as it is practised in all the Western democracies. Why must this practice be inaccessible for Quebec? Curiously enough, this charge is usually accompanied, as in *Le Canada face à son destin*, by lengthy expositions on how the rest of Canada should proceed, in the event of a negotiation between equals with Quebec, to keep its own cake by giving an impression of sincerity while actually remaining implacable.

The English-Canadian elites have a gut inability to accept Quebec as a place where autonomous political power can be used, with all that involves of stakes, risks, and promises. There is a strong temptation to sink into a rather too elementary psychology and see this refusal by English Canada as reflecting its own inability.

It is not out of the question that political realism and the possibility of real success may have aroused this animosity toward the sovereignty association formula. This formula involves a message of power, negotiation, and compromise. One prefers the purity of the independentist option, though its chances are well known to be minimal. The dream before reality!

Is It a Write-off?

Whether Quebec is central to English Canada's concerns or merely on the periphery, it represents an object that English Canada cannot yet discern in its full extent and in all its ramifications. By turns, Quebec is seen as province, culture, region, minority, though never as a political society with its own structures, risks, actors, and logic. Unable to define itself as a society, English Canada finds it hard to extend this treatment to Quebec.

In this context, it is understandable that there have never been Quebec-Canada negotiations. Negotiations are essentially a structure of the mind, a means for Quebec to take its dreams of equality for its reality as a province. The idea of "a Quebec that demands" and "an English Canada that says no" is thus far from corresponding to reality. As we have seen, Quebec has never asked for anything and English Canada has never been present. In these circumstances, can there still be talk of a dialogue of the deaf?

A Quebec-Canada negotiation is unthinkable, no matter on what basis for discussion. As far as the rest of the country is concerned, there has never been a Quebec-Canada constitutional file. Depending on moods and moments, English-Canadians have preferred to see:

- a family squabble between French-Canadians (Trudeau versus Lévesque);
- a language conflict between francophones and anglophones;
- a conflict of powers between a provincial government and the federal government;
- a conflict between a poor province and some rich provinces; or
- the traditional rivalry between the two biggest provinces.

None of these definitions of the "Quebec problem" involve a conflict between two societies.

Not only has such negotiation never taken place but it never will be able to take place. Here is what Smiley thinks of this:

> In some of the revisionist writings, it appears that the major impulse to English-Canadian nationhood should be to interact more constructively

with Quebec. Yet is seems to me patently unrealistic to expect the larger of the two communities to change its organization and ideology for the sole reasons that this will bring about better relations with the smaller. To use an analogy . . . the cause of Christian ecumenism might well be furthered if the denominations of the World Council of Churches united themselves under a common hierarchy which would associate with the Vatican. Yet if Baptists and Presbyterians consented to this they would cease in any definable way to be Baptists or Presbyterians (Smiley, 1967, p. 155).

We are going to have to think about something other than this impossible negotiation. However, before thinking about the possible, let us proceed to think the unthinkable.

Part II

A Prospective on Quebec-Canada Relations

Chapter 5

The Break: *The Judicial Environment of a Biased Scenario*

It is relatively easy to show that the apocalyptic scenarios which emerged after the constitutional developments of 1982 had no foundation. The *Constitution Act, 1982* represents a serious political defeat for Quebec, but this loss is no more irreversible than it is immediate. Besides, it is not impossible to think that the act might serve Quebec's own interests one day. After all, since we have already witnessed one complete reversal from initial expectations in this legislation, it is not beyond the wit of man to imagine others just as unpredictable. But is an undramatized scenario still a scenario?

An Act Is an Act

Although we must avoid being (too) dramatic or dwelling too much on the future of the French language in Canada and the French culture in Quebec, it cannot be denied that the year 1982 was a significant turning point in the political relationship between Quebec and the rest of Canada. It does not actually matter if Quebec's defeat was real or imaginary, temporary or permanent, accidental or premeditated: it was perceived as serious by broad sections of the Quebec population. Yet we must not exaggerate the extent or intensity of a dissatisfaction that was the prerogative of those who actively participated in the political process; and in Quebec, as elsewhere, this is always a minority.

The passage of the *Constitution Act, 1982* did not send the citizens running into the streets. Nor was the government anticipating vast movements of civil disobedience. Quebec City quite simply chose not to sign the constitutional agreement, rejecting both its letter and its spirit. It is the exclusive privilege of a minority power to say no, sometimes to its very freedom, but most often to attempts by the majority to rationalize the political environment. The readiness with which this passive resistance was organized showed the type of political culture that had been allowed to develop in Canada. It was really not expected that things would occur to everyone's satisfaction. The choice, therefore, was to stick with the tried and true scenario. The choice was to pretend.

The virtually total absence of reaction in the rest of Canada to Quebec's refusal to accept this method said much about the lack of vision in English Canada. No one pointed out that Quebec's refusal amounted to a *de facto* veto, and one that gained in significance by the fact that the courts had carefully stipulated that no judicial basis for such a veto existed. Here was an unlooked-for opportunity to rebuild the Canadian political process, based on the acknowledged equality between the two founding peoples. If the governments of English Canada finally let this opportunity slip and chose to see nothing "different" in Quebec's refusal, that was one thing; but the fact that no one, not one party in a Canadian province and not a single member of a legislative assembly signified disagreement, that was quite another thing.

One could never say enough about the deep revulsion this attitude aroused in a good many Québécois of all political stripes. Apparently, English-Canadians found this disgust incomprehensible. It had to be one thing or the other; or perhaps they saw the *Constitution Act, 1982* as unimportant and felt that there was no reason to be so upset about it; or maybe it was Quebec that they thought unimportant.

In the end, it was not so much a matter of disgust as of sadness. So this was the English Canada with which Quebec liked to proclaim equality! Was it really worth it?

In certain circles, this passiveness in the government and population was misread as a vote of censure by the citizens. Various polls, in fact, established that a steadily rising number of these citizens thought the government should have signed and should now sign the constitutional accord. But should we be surprised by this at a time when Quebec was experiencing its worst economic crisis and when the integrity of several of its new institutions was being threatened? Hoping to build a country on the indifference and sagging confidence of a large proportion of its citizens is not a very good omen. Here already was a sign that people were resigning themselves to quiet mediocrity.

When looked at prospectively, the constitutional agreement of 1981 bore all the signs of what is usually termed a "rupture." Yet what was broken? If no true negotiations took place between Quebec and Canada, can we actually speak of a rupture in negotiations and the failure of a process — the rupture of an equal partnership that never existed, of an attempt by Quebec to gain equality? By definition, an attempt is a trial: it cannot really be broken.

And a rupture with what results? What will be the concrete effects of the political normalization of Quebec that I mentioned? How will this mediocrity be expressed in economic, cultural, and social terms? Everyone in Canada could be affected, but will everyone be affected on the same basis and with the same consequences? Can we really speak of catastrophe in the case of a normalization that is bound to have the advantage of putting an end to uncertainty and tension? One cannot be "normal" and "worried" at the same time! Will the citizens actually be the first who are penalized in this new political context?

As soon as we leave the all-too-comfortable ground of our prospective policy, its only purpose being to alarm or please, the job grows more complex. There is a danger of slipping into banalities or dodging discussion by the repetition of "on the one hand . . . but on the other hand": this may help the prospectivist cover his rear, but it does nothing to help the debate along. Accordingly, I shall introduce this scenario by sticking as closely as possible to the new judicial reality whose outline can already be perceived. After that, I shall consider the development of Canadian federalism since 1945, with emphasis on decentralization and the regionalization of decision centres. In this chapter, I shall be looking particularly at the new judicial environment, while the focus of the following chapter will be the Canadian political dynamic.

In short, I want to combine ancient and modern, new and old, the judicial and the political. I am well aware that this is not a very ambitious program of prospection. I shall be passing over a good number of important realities, such as the economy and the new world order.

One must avoid using this view of the future to lend style where there is none. Naturally, discussion of quiet mediocrity as the chief menace lacks the excitement of describing clearcut dangers coming from outside. The imaginary challenges brought in by the fourth wave are always more enticing than old, unsolved problems. Is there any need to state that by arranging the Canadian reality of coming years around these two axes, I am not doing justice to its complexity? Well, there is no justice in politics, either.

Let me sum up the essence of my argument straightaway: the effects of the *Constitution Act, 1982* can only be assessed in terms of the double process that has shaped Canadian development for more than twenty years — increasing political standardization and accelerating deterioration of the Canadian economic environment. I believe that these two processes are connected.

Strictly speaking, then, rather than a rupture in 1982, there was an actualization of certain forces which had been at work in Canadian society for half a century, coupled with a redefinition of a number of rules of play in order to bring them more in line with this underlying trend. The essential thing right now is to pull the *Constitution Act, 1982* down a peg or two. Not too far, though: we have so few pan-Canadian symbols that we can differ on this cheerfully.

The act is banal in the sense that, like all laws, decrees, charters, and constitutions, it is better understood in terms of the immediate past than of the future that is to be created by it. It put the official stamp on a development that had already largely taken place. So many deals and compromises presided at its birth that one would hardly expect to find the originality needed for a rupture. This act is the image of problems that Canadians have failed to confront and resolve.

Yet this act also opens doors — not to a future that will be radically different from the past but to one that will reproduce with greater fidelity a past that was already very heavy indeed. In this sense, the *Constitution Act, 1982* preciously preserves for future generations the seeds of the problems that attended its passage. One could even say that it is giving them new life. The act is liable to aggravate the centralizing and standardizing process already at work in the Canadian federation and thus to accentuate the federation's inability to act and reverse its dependence. A token of Canadian impotence, it helps us calm our future impotence. After a charge like this, an explanation is called for!

A New Power: Interpretation

Much has been made of the enormous power that judges would have in codifying the rules of the Canadian political game. One of the main arguments of the English-Canadian provinces against the entrenchment of rights in the Canadian Constitution rested on just this concern. There has been talk of a government of judges, of hobbling the executive, of the abduction of parliamentary democracy and, above all, of the inclusion of an unpredictable new element in Canadian politics. These are real dangers, but they are also inevitable in any attempt at reforming collective institutions. Such a process always produces winners and losers, and the latter are rarely the same ones as before. Must we not expect this more or less, since the need was felt to change these institutions? If one knows the inertia of such bodies, and the weight their organizational culture assumes, it is not surprising that when changes finally do come, they alter behaviour considerably.

Although readily imagined, the route that interpretation of this new constitutional document will follow cannot be foreseen with any certainty. All that is needed, for example, is for the judges to interpret the *Canadian Charter of Rights and Freedoms* in a particular way, and everything is called into doubt. The logic of the separation of powers itself often pushes the courts to show "originality" in their rulings, more originality, at least, than the legislative imagined and the executive would have liked. In addition, the judiciary power cannot have the unity of thought and action that characterizes a government. It is more subject to the personalities of the men and women, judges and others, who comprise it. For example, the court only has to rule that the idea of "collective right" falls within the definition of basic rights and the possibility of Quebec's independence becomes a judicial reality: it is then possible to remodel Quebec's — and Canada's — collective landscape from top to bottom, in ways that even the most extreme supporters of Quebec sovereignty or Canadian independence had never considered. So we can expect anything, including the worst, as well as whatever misfortune chance throws our way.

The turn that judicial interpretation may take is not as worrying for the political future of Canada and Quebec as certain changes that this Charter will bring into political relations in Canada. To the naked eye, these changes are imperceptible. They upset nothing in the immediate future. Their effect is real, however, and it is cumulative.

It is hardly original to point out that the problem of constitutionalizing a charter of rights is essentially American in origin. The same may be true of its application. Only in the United States do we find this combination of a federal system coupled with a Bill of Rights that is as binding on the interpretation of the courts. Canada's constitutional "liberation" from Britain could thus only be accomplished by an act of the British Parliament, following a trail blazed by the United States.

The influence of the *Constitution Act, 1982* does not stop with its substance or with the way the act was applied. On these effects, everything, or virtually everything, has already been said. As far as both the act's content and its application go, these were major setbacks for Quebec and for its collective institutions in orienting the development of Quebec society in any given direction.

We must also look closely, however, at the judicial argument by which the Supreme Court approved the legality of the federal move. Up to the present, the main concern has been to understand the logic of this argument and to assess its quality. There has been little attempt to measure the effect, not of the ruling itself but of the reasoning on which it rests. Yet it is readily seen that this reasoning will play a considerable role in future interpretations by the courts. The judges will at least want to rely on what they have already said on the subject. Coherence requires this.

In this respect, the majority opinion of the Supreme Court judges in the celebrated ruling is food for thought. The judges' definition of the question before them was strange, to say the least:

> What is central here is the untrammelled authority at law of the two federal Houses to proceed as they wish in the management of their own procedures and hence to adopt the Resolution which is intended for submission to Her Majesty for action thereon by the United Kingdom Parliament (p. 62).[1]

By dwelling on this "untrammelled authority . . . to proceed as they wish in . . . their own procedures," the court oriented the entire discussion toward the principle of parliamentary supremacy, though that supremacy was nowhere questioned by the appellants. Once the question had been put in terms of the supremacy of Parliament, rather than in terms of sharing the supremacy between two parliamentary orders, the die was cast. From that moment on, the position of the provinces did not have a chance.

There followed a definitive affirmation, the first to be so clear, of the supremacy of the federal Parliament; for not only did the judges reply to a question that was not put to them in the same terms, but they also rejected a claim that had not been lodged, namely that the provinces were trying to impose their "supremacy vis-a-vis the federal Parliament" (p. 44). On this claim, the judges held that "the exclusiveness of the provincial powers . . . cannot be gainsaid" (p. 44). Thus, a federal claim which had never been expressed was supported at the expense of a provincial claim which had never been explicity advanced. This curious procedure confirms the unpredictability of the action of the courts, which I mentioned earlier.

After this, the supremacy of the federal Parliament was more important in the Canadian political system than the prerogatives of the provinces. By comparison with some past decisions, especially the 1937 decision on labour laws and the 1951 decision on the division of powers, this was not only a complete reversal but also a most explicit reversal. In a debate which in every detail resembled the classic confrontations of Alexander Hamilton and James Madison, the Supreme Court of Canada was taking a clear stand against the vision of two equal, coordinated and co-independent orders of government.

Until then, Canadian sovereignty and federalism had always been treated as such overlapping questions that the one could not be discussed without bringing in the other. Canada existed because it was a federation. This was its lot, or its misfortune as some would say. In 1867 and 1931, when Canadian sovereignty came up, one referred necessarily to the federal character of Canada. The ruling of September 1981 put an end to this association. It spelled a significant shift in perspective, a shift that was far more important than the blessing for the legality of Ottawa's plan, which had been the reason for the debate.

This was not simply a matter of a victory for a centralizing vision of Canada. Such victories often have no political sequel. But here was an affirmation that the centralizing vision, or more specifically the view of the central government, was the only one that coincided with Canadian sovereignty. The federal character of Canada was not changed by this. What was changed was the definition of this federalism, which thereafter belonged wholly to the central government, which was now considered to be the sole depositary of Canadian sovereignty.

The very notion of federalism was disappearing as a political arche-type. The focus moved now to the enormous variety with which this formula was applied around the world: "There is not and cannot be any standardized federal system from which particular conclusions must necessarily be drawn (p. 49).

A political scientist will not object, of course, to a court's recognizing a certain priority to political reality over constitutional law, but if one cannot and must not take anything away from the concept of federalism, the latter no longer has much value. The following comment by a constitutionalist from California deserves to be quoted at length:

> As they say, if you can believe that, you can believe anything. Either real federalism has certain common characteristics which are reflective in all federal systems and at least is reflective of one or more theoretical models or there is no such thing as theoretical or actual federalism. One cannot have one without the other. The idea that reality is determined by examining empirical facts from which flexible and variable principles are drawn for temporary use only is a pragmatist's delusion! The Court's majority must answer how many forms of federalism can be maintained over the long haul if its principle of federal paramountcy, . . . given the present Court decisions on a matter so important to the Canadian federation . . . were to prevail in a series of precedent cases. The consequence must necessarily be centralism and not federalism (Layson, 1981, p. 35).

This shift in perspective would undoubtedly be more important for Canada's political future than all the specific rulings the courts could produce. From this point on, it would be impossible for the federal government to do anything that ran counter to Canadian federalism, since all that would be needed was recognition that the action was consistent with the original character of the federal system. Should the federal government decide to do away with Canada's federal character altogether, in all likelihood the courts would object. The question, however, would certainly not present itself in these terms. The constitu-tional nibbling away of legislative powers, which had not ceased since 1945, would be aided and even encouraged by the change.

Something New in Canada

It is hard to foresee how Canada's judicial structure will develop in the coming years. Nonetheless, this is what I have attempted to do. What comes out of these few remarks is not so much the threats posed by the judicial provisions of the *Canadian Charter of Rights and Freedoms*. We can only congratulate ourselves on a measure that enlarges the freedom of individuals in relation to the state, even though there are questions to be asked concerning the somewhat mystifying nature of this effort. Was it really necessary to curtail the freedom of the provincial, regional, and national collectivities that make up Canada? This is the prime question. It has to be one thing or the other (or so I am tempted to conclude yet again): either this operation was actually necessary — and this tells us a lot about the political concordat that joins the country's various components together — or else it was not really necessary. In the latter case, why resign oneself to it?

In a country that suffers a lack of autonomy, was it necessary to undermine one of the most important areas, the political and judicial sphere of Quebec, on the pretext of standardization? Will this downward levelling process truly benefit Canadians? Does it better protect the rights of the citizen to diminish the autonomy of the intermediate collective spheres? Has Canada, which should be seeking differences and distinctions in all things, gained at all from this standardization of the judicial sphere?

How are we to ensure that a political dynamic, which also is autonomous, is maintained if everything that made Canada unique is eliminated? Until now, Canadian politics has enjoyed a life and a dynamic of its own. It has constantly been creating its own development. Politics is what has kept Canada "alive," and a captivating life it was, to say the least. The judiciary and its insistence on norms and standardization had very little to do with this process. Fortunately, I might add. And now there has been a decision to reverse the order of things.

Chapter 6

Canada the Cold: *The Political Dynamic of a Biased Scenario*

Let us first see what the situation is. Compared with the promises whose fulfilment could reasonably be foreseen in the mid-1960s, the Canada of today seems bogged down in an endless cycle of indifference and mediocrity. Yet compared with other countries, it is still in an enviable situation, and the rumours of its impending death are greatly exaggerated. This diagnosis of mine has to be trenchant, for Canadian literature is overflowing with analyses so full of nuance that one ends up convinced that the patient is indeed dying, but is in good health just the same. This diagnosis is my point of departure for our scenario. This is the Canada I shall talk about, for this is the Canada out of which the immediate future will be made.

A Constitution in the Avant-garde of Delay

The Canadian Constitution is not adjusted for the requirements which the end of the century imposes on political entities. This statement will surprise no one. Is it still worth making? Probably not, except to point out how hard it is to switch this maladjustment into a state of emergency. The inability to give way to constitutional panic speaks eloquently of the genuine importance of these documents. It also tells us about the host of ways that have always been available for Canadians to escape the weakness of their Constitution. People have often chosen to see this way of doing things as a sign of Canadian political ingenuity. Perhaps one should also regard it as the result of particularly favourable conditions.

In a time of economic expansion and growth in the functions of government, it is always relatively easy to disregard the official rules. Reality itself often obliges us to do this. The situation grows complicated when the day comes when certain players feel the need to invoke the rules to safeguard or increase their bids. This is when there can no longer be pretence that the Constitution does not exist.

In this regard, the government's decision in the spring of 1975 to impose constitutional changes at any cost indicated a sudden realization that things could not continue as before. For the first time, Ottawa needed a new constitution, or at least thought that it did. Automatically, Quebec felt the need for constitutional guarantees. In this connection, one should remember Robert Bourassa's reply to Pierre Trudeau in the summer of 1975. The same reaction was heard from the Atlantic provinces over equalization and from the West about natural resources. All of a sudden, the Constitution ceased being a luxury and became a necessity. In the Canadian case, it can hardly be said that necessity was the mother of invention; not in the constitutional field, at any rate.

In 1982 the country had a unique opportunity to adjust the Constitution to Canada's new geopolitical situations, and also to update some political symbols. The choice was made not to do this. Canada remained a constitutional monarchy without a monarch, one of the few political societies, along with Tonga, to choose the monarchical system again when there was a beautiful chance to break with the past. Although the time was propitious for redefining the country's reason for existence, the choice was to keep the definition given in the preamble of the *Constitution Act, 1867*, namely "to promote the interests of the British Empire." The decision to continue to use this device of the British parliament revealed more than a simple desire to show some constitutional continuity; it revealed the inability of those who made it to anticipate what the reaction of Canadians would be. In the opinion of the minister of justice himself, they preferred "not to be drawn into useless battles where we would never have seen the end and which finally would have served only the interests of the Quebec separatists" (*La Presse*, January 16, 1982).

Let us recall once more, for the record, that this new constitution, which provides for a formula of constitutional amendment that ought to make it more adaptable, is already the subject of cases before the courts, so that they can stipulate what the document really means. The ink is not yet dry and already we must try to decipher the writing. Here is a form of originality and creativity that the country could well do without. One could almost speak of planned constitutional obsolescence. Canada has given itself a constitutional Edsel!

This obsolescence is the best possible guarantee of the permanence of the constitutional file. There would be no point in denying it priority and returning it to the back shelf; this item would refuse to die. Nothing has been resolved, and the conflicts of powers will not disappear. It is even predictable that the courts, busy with the application of the *Canadian Charter of Rights and Freedoms*, will not be too enthusiastic about the notion of arbitrating conflicts between levels of government as well.

In contrast to the years 1963–65, it was neither electoral motives nor the nationalist dynamic that forced the opening of a constitutional construction site this time. More important was the fact that nothing had been dealt with in this domain for some 20 years. In addition, the new political priority which the federal government avidly took for its own, helped by the judicial priority conferred on it by the Charter, would aggravate the conflicts. For the provinces, it would be a question of defending acquisitions that had never been confirmed by a new division of legislative responsibilities. The struggle is always more intense when one's back is to the wall.

The Quiet Ukrainization

With the collapse of the Third Option, Canada found itself without any great prospects as far as its role in the international community was concerned. Simply expressing interest in an issue and placing it in the exclusive domain of the prime minister, does not ensure automatic top drawer attention. Theatrical flair and spectacular moves are fated to remain without sequel if they have no basis in solid fact. Canada's economic and cultural domination by the United States and the similarity in their views on all the great international questions are permanent factors that make it hard to develop a position that is original, effective, and not contrived.

From this standpoint, Canada has all the geopolitical disadvantages of Finland, without having Finland's advantages: participation in a community that is ideologically different from that of its powerful neighbour; encouragement from fellow members of the community to maintain this difference; and a socioeconomic organization and culture which differ greatly from those of its neighbour. Too small and too big at the same time, Canada cannot hope to go unnoticed. It seems to be doomed to an unending effort to distinguish itself from the United States so that it can establish credibility in international forums in which it often owes its presence to the Americans.

This "Ukrainization" of Canada could be more pronounced by the end of the century. What holds it back a little is the interest that the United States and the other great powers have in the presence of an entity right next to the Americans. But is this a satisfying role for Canada? Still, it is the only one that seems to interest us. (Could it be the only one available?) To play a role on the international stage, and not just to dwell endlessly on Canada's distinct character, we must have something to say and not simply interests to protect.

It is in the cultural area that this Canadian silence is the most obvious and the most tragic. The problems and eventual fate of pay television are an example of the cultural destiny that haunts the country. During all the years when we had the "privilege of historical lag" and could watch the United States grappling with the start-up problems of this new cultural industry, debate in Canada was limited to whether the industry would only abet the Americanization of the airwaves, or whether it could help the country achieve cultural autonomy by giving the French element in Canadian culture the market that it had always lacked and by giving the anglophone element a previously unavailable window on a specific area. Today, it seems plausible to think that neither of these scenarios will come to pass.

Simply in terms of expectations, there is something awesome in so swift a collapse. It tells us a lot about how sparse our knowledge of the cultural environment of Canadians is, and in this case the misreading has been costly. Yet pay television is here to stay. The very fact that, despite initial reservations, it was allowed in on the grounds that progress cannot be stopped and that an orderly introduction would be preferable to piracy (probably a realistic assessment) shows just how little man-oeuvring room the political authorities have. In addition, there are early indications that the accelerated Americanization of the Canadian air-waves will also not take place, at least not in so cavalier a manner. Given the increased fragmentation of markets in the United States, Americans can now welcome various types of programming. This is not the case in Canada, where we have to expect not just Americanization but Amer-icanization from the bottom up, which in the long run only makes it more difficult for Canadian artists to advance themselves and their style; unless, of course, the style is a bilingual version of what is beamed to us from the south.

This unjust assessment, which takes no account of Telidon, the space arm, or the LRT train, applies generally to Quebec. The details need adjusting, but the spirit of the diagnosis remains the same. In certain areas, Quebec seems to be ahead, though not always in the right way. In others, it lags behind. One subject, however, is peculiar to Quebec: demography. I shall return to this at length later on.

It will have been noticed that my diagnosis has very little connection with the economy. Yet if there is a sector in which Canadian misfortunes are particularly well documented, this is it. Ever since 1970, Canada's competitive position has done nothing but deteriorate, to the point where no one now dares to mention the country's place on the interna-tional scale of living standards. Gone are the days when every Canadian schoolboy rehearsed to anyone who would listen that famous tag about the "second-highest standard of living in the world." Although lacking the human resources to control the technological take-off, Canada still possesses an industrial structure that will help greatly in bargaining for a piece of it. Already, there are signs of profound changes in the organiza-tion of the workplace (computerization, robotization), all of which sup-port the prediction that there will be lower levels of employment, though without this loss being compensated for by the entry of new sectors that would allow the country to rid itself of U.S. economic domination. We are already witnessing a movement of imitation in the Canadian economy, except that this new economy of ours will very likely operate at a slightly lower level than the original.

The schizophrenia in official economic parlance is remarkable. On the one hand, there is continual emphasis on the important role Canada plays on the international economic scene: summits of industrialized nations, GATT, IMF, North-South dialogue. . . . On the other hand, economists like to depress themselves with talk of our falling productivity, falling investments, falling dollar, and so on. One ends up believing that the fundamental source of all our problems is economic. "We have lost too much time over the Constitution and Quebec. We have to get to the real problems." This has emerged as the official chorus of Canada's political anthem, replacing federalism on our collective agenda.

It is not easy to characterize Canadian federalism these days. Since 1970, it seems to have lost its inner dynamic. It is not creative now; it waits to be interpreted. Its questioning has lost intensity and has been replaced by nothing. It is simply there, an integral part of the political landscape, and tends more and more to blend right into it.

It was really not so long ago when every social change, every technological innovation had immediate repercussions on the functioning of federalism. Think of the upheavals caused, for instance, by the coming of the welfare state or, more recently, by cable television and satellites. For several years now, Canadian federalism has let itself be pulled along. One feels that it has come to the end of the possibilities of its originality. It contents itself with clichés about its character — decentralizer, executive, or quasi-diplomat.

Let us abandon this assessment, however, to look at the causes of this Canadian evil. There could be no question of adding yet another analysis of the reasons for our predicament. The list is already so impressive that one more might go unperceived. Not only is the list bristling with details, but it also enjoys such broad support in Canadian society that we could almost speak of unanimity. So let us go straight to the heart of the Canadian consensus.

A Lone Villain: Division

"If things are going badly in Canada, it is because Canadians are divided." This sentence has now achieved the status of an official motto. Who would dream of questioning it? In some situations, it is used to describe the past: "It was when Canadians were divided that they failed." In others, it is applied to a dreaded future: "If Canadians continue to be divided in this way, they will be incapable of facing the challenges of tomorrow." There is a very rich vocabulary for depicting these divisions. We meet "a people turned against itself," involved in "sterile conflicts" (in Canada, conflicts are always sterile), whose "costly confrontations" are legion, holding them back from "self-real-ization." We hear of divisions between east and west, north and south, francophones and anglophones, employers and workers, federal and provincial governments, rich and poor, whites and visible minorities, employed and unemployed, new technologies and old industries, men and women, young and old. The list seems endless, and it is well understood that the Quebec-Canada split occupies only one place among many.

There is always a common enemy somewhere around who summons Canadians from both sides of a disagreement to shelve their differences: if only the bosses and the unions could get together and really go after the problem of productivity; if only union workers and other workers would band together to prevent technological changes from destroying jobs; if only the Québécois, and especially PQ supporters, would join forces with the federal government to make some progress regarding the rights of francophones in the West; if only the left of English Canada could combine with the social democrats of Quebec; if only. . . .

This is not the place to embark on a sociological piece about Canada's fascination with unity and its insistence that this unity should be fash-ioned in diversity (on condition that the diversity is appropriately uni-form and is lived the same way at the same time everywhere in the country). This obsession with symmetry is not unrelated to the spatial representations Canadians make of their country — that rectangle har-moniously divided in two lengthwise, and divided into equal parts from top to bottom. I really must do an essay on Canada's political topology one day.

For almost half a century, an imposing lexicon has been building up, especially in English Canada, to convey one facet or another of what has undoubtedly become one of the most serene certainties about Canada, namely its decentralized character. Canada is apparently the most decentralized country on this planet. It is thus that we speak of provin-cialism, province-building, provincial autonomy, and regionalism. All these terms veil slightly differing realities which we are unfortunately not able to explore here. It will be noted, however, how unanimously Canada's various scientific traditions have come out in favour of an ineluctable tendency toward provincialism in Canada. This tendency arouses many fears, especially in English Canada, and the use of terms like balkanization and disintegration is the most obvious symptom of this. In Quebec, the debate has not arisen in the same terms, and the conditions in which federalism has been experienced there have pre-cluded this negative view.

It is hardly surprising that the English-Canadian social scientists, working in the various dominant traditions in the study of Canadian society, should share this view. Economists, for whom the market is the ultimate analytical tool, cannot avoid taking an interest in everything that interferes with the harmonious operation of this market. Nor can political scientists, concerned with electoral behaviour, avoid viewing the electoral market from a national perspective and trying to measure the influence of the different "little homelands." For researchers of liberal bent (these terms are used here with a fair degree of latitude) this provincialism can only lead to sectarianism, since, by definition, it offers a more limiting view of reality. For those of more conservative inclinations, provincialism is necessarily an obstacle to the installation of a Canadian nationality.

To a liberal-minded intellectual in English Canada, it is apparently impossible for anyone who operates in a provincial setting to take a progressive attitude to social issues or to have respect for civil liberties and concern for justice and equal opportunity. On the other hand, the conservative-minded suspects that provincialism leads to increased bureaucratization of social relations and to an increase in the modern state's intervention in personal lives. Both, of course, have honeyed and deferential words for local democracy, any control by the grassroots, and respect for regional characteristics, but there could never be a question of putting this local practice into a permanent political structure.

Where the unanimity becomes more surprising is with the discovery that it also embraces the participants in the old tradition of political economy. I have already discussed Quebec's place in this tradition at some length. I shall not be returning to this question for the moment, but I do wish to note how far this group, too, is convinced of the rise of provincialism and of the inevitable dangers to which this exposes Canada. The arguments exist in infinite variety. Some deserve mention:

- According to Stevenson (1979), it was the provincial hold on natural resources that automatically produced this provincialist bias. So long as this hold is maintained, the integration of the Canadian economy and society will be impossible.
- According to Laxer (1974), it is mainly the oil multinationals that profit from provincialism. Canada's political and economic independence, then, is going through an adjustment to this provincialism.
- For Levitt (1970), provincialism is only the most recent form of Canadian capitulation to the continental economic domination of the United States.
- Numerous versions of this argument will be found in the writings of Stevenson, who has let it be known that the variations in Canadian regionalism are actually reflections of regional changes in the United States or, again, that provincialism has served as a power vehicle for certain class groups (1979).
- According to Armstrong (1981), the conflicts between the different levels of government and the attempts by certain provinces, including Ontario, to form themselves into political and economic areas are

largely explained by the interests of the various economic groups in the country that amuse themselves by playing one government against the other.

The positive aspects of regionalism are rarely mentioned, the exceptions being Ryerson's work on the origins of Confederation and that of R.T. Taylor (1975) on the business world. Taylor advances the hypothesis that the attempts at centralization and unification found in the *Constitution Act, 1867* blocked the development of more progressive social and economic policies. On occasion, there is work, well carried out, which completely omits to address the political factor. This is generally the case with research that uses the theory of "basic products." For example, in John McCallum's fascinating study (1980) of the origins of economic disparity between Quebec and Ontario, which covers the period 1850–70, he forgets to mention even the word "Confederation." The study is all about transportation networks, farming technology, urban distribution, and climatic conditions. No matter how hard one looks, there is no connection to be found between these factors and the political project of federalism.

In the Atlantic provinces, the recent resurgence of interest in the "development of the underdevelopment" of the region has encouraged hope for an investigation of the so-called advantages of economic centralization and political unification. Such charges are to be found in the work of Forbes (1979), Alexander (1983), Bercuson (1977) and Mathews (1983), to mention only the latest. Although the prosecution's case is long and detailed, however, the verdict is never delivered. Mathews, for example, after a magisterial exposé of the sins of the policies of regional expansion (which instead of solving the problem, turn what used to be regional disparity into regional dependence), concludes: "A country as big and as regionally diverse as Canada must have regional planning if it is to fulfil its social and economic potential" (Mathews, 1983, p. 220). To achieve this, he suggests, all that is needed is for this regional expansion policy to overcome its current crisis of legitimacy.

Nowhere is this inability to make logical conclusions and to challenge the evidence more poignant than in David Alexander's writings about Newfoundland. In one of his last publications before his death, he came out in favour of Lord Acton's view that "big is beautiful":

People are better off in large and diverse countries than in small and homogeneous ones . . . [since] it obliges tolerance, cultivates creativity, and provides the scale sometimes needed to face otherwise overwhelming problems (Alexander, 1983, p. 96).

The resemblance here to the views of Pierre Trudeau is striking. Given Alexander's analysis of Newfoundland's underdevelopment, his study has some surprising things in it: Canada's problem is both simple and complex; it is a question of myths, and since in this domain big myths are better than little myths, in terms of the happiness they offer, the federal government's mission is all laid out for it:

> Canada is a country with provincial myths, but no country-wide ones which are seriously believed. We settled half a continent but the Americans did it first and the imagery of the feat is theirs. We claimed independence from the British Empire only to relinquish it to the successor, and in neither case with a struggle. We created a more equitable society out of economic growth, but it was not a unique moral feat. We said for a time that we were a bilingual, binational state in the New World; now we learn that we are not. The country is void of the unique historical accomplishments which are the foundation for myths that render enduring attachment. In such a void people no longer complacent or quiescent may turn to the exclusive cultivation of provincial myths as a means of finding Acton's "new notion of happiness." The trouble is that the resulting happiness may not be as substantial as the notion (Alexander, 1983, pp. 96–97).

Provincialism unquestionably gets a bad press in English Canada, even from those whose analysis obliges them to conclude that it is the policies promoted by the federal government, usually for the benefit of the centre of the country, that have created the chronic underdevelopment of some regions.

Although provincialism gets a poor press by left and right alike, in the centre as on the periphery, everyone agrees that Canada, from its beginnings, has developed through cycles of centralization and decentralization. For reasons that have as much to do with the sociology of science as with reality, this centralizing-decentralizing perspective on Canadian federalism has always been the dominant one. The diagnoses and remedies offered for Canadian problems always turn on this axis.

Decentralization? What Decentralization?

This way of looking at the Canadian political reality simply reflects a vision of politics that is essentially judicial and historical. It has very little room for the relations between economics and politics. When it comes right down to it, the Canadian economy is well or badly run as a result of political decisions. In this way, the traditional equation is completely overthrown. Ironically, Canada is without any doubt the place where politics won its independence most quickly from an economics that is reduced to demanding recognition for its relative autonomy. Marx did not foresee this curious reversal and the victory of politics in a dominion of the British Empire.

In this regard, the *Constitution Act, 1982* can be seen as the revenge of economics on politics. In fact, three of the act's most important elements, namely those related to free movement, equalization, and natural resources, have an essentially economic flavour. There can surely be no coincidence in the fact that, of the thirty or so questions which appeared at one time or another on the agenda of constitutional discussions, it was these three that found places in the final document, though they had not even been part of the political scene back in 1965. There is no end of irony in seeing these economic considerations turn up in a political document under cover of a charter of individual rights. For example, the right of free movement assures all Canadians in the poorer regions that they can follow capital when it relocates in more profitable regions. Here is a right of internal immigration, by which the country's internal underdevelopment and colonialism can be organized on a more solid basis. The status of refugee looking for work is made official. Even the most fiery campaigners for manpower mobility were not asking this much.

As soon as we move away from the judicial forms of the division of legislative powers between Canada's two levels of government and look at the causes that presided over the creation and development of the state structure, in whatever phase of its activity, the picture changes altogether. Whether in its "constitutional review" version or that of "federal-provincial conflicts", Canadian politics loses a certain amount of its mysterious specificity.

The Canadian social formation is characterized by the presence of political institutions and mechanisms which are there to give meaning to the spatial insertion of social groups and modes of economic organization that define Canada at any given time. Historians have pointed out the weakness of this economic equation, especially as regards the bourgeoisie of commerce and banking at a time, 1850, when it was becoming imperative to proceed with the rearrangment of the localized economic areas to the north of the American republic. In Canada, the unification of these colonial areas was carried out under pressure more from outside events than from a national bourgeoisie that would thus have seized the opportunity to secure its grasp on a political and cultural hegemony. The creation of the legal country was thus not the hallowing of any historic compromise, and still less was it the outcome of mass movements or the victory of one social group over others. Because they were not challenged or threatened, the pre-existing social groups did not disappear with unification of the Canadian political and economic area. What would eventually be known as the dual dimension of the Canadian political crisis — national as far as Quebec was concerned, and regional in the other subnational areas — existed already in 1867. In varying guises, it has easily held its own ever since. Here is how Gilles Bourque sums up the conditions that have prevented the positioning of the usual sequence:

National ruling bourgeoisie
↓
Integrated social bloc
↓
Political and ideological hegemony

Canada, then, is the product of a merging effected by steam, which is hardly a play on words . . . Lacking a true adversary, deprived of a pre-capitalist ruling class that could have resisted the creation of the national state, without a colonial power refusing its national liberation, the Canadian bourgeoisie found itself cut off from a mother country, which made a "concession" barely asked for. The conditions for establishing a true Canadian social bloc would be a matter for people of the world, matters negotiated in the creation of a bloc in power, but a very special bloc in power in which the hegemonized segments of the ruling classes could rely on social blocs that were already spatialized (former colonies or former districts within these colonies), taken thereafter as regional and/or national (Bourque and Duchastel, 1983, p. 138; translation).

Until 1930, this absence of hegemonic control meant that Canada remained in relatively stable balance between its basic structural unity and the various tendencies to rupture that ran through it now and again. With no marked presence on the part of the state, questions of the division of legislative powers in the Canadian state were of small importance. One could then speak of two levels of government that were autonomous and without points of contact.

Things changed rapidly from the 1930s on. Given the extent of the economic crisis and its unprecedented social repercussions, an attempt was launched to find an explanation, or rather, to apply to Canada the various Keynesian explanations which were then beginning to circulate. It was thus that the Royal Commission on Wage and Price Controls came to speak of underconsumption and, in order to stimulate consumption, of the need to harmonize labour policies by setting minimum wage levels and remuneration according to sector. Here was the first diagnosis of "the Canadian evil" in terms of areas of economic activity which were too independent of one another. By a curious reasoning, the commissioners suggested active intervention by the central government, which alone had the capacity to impose the national uniformity called for by the reliance of Canada's prosperity on world markets in which prices were set for the export of certain basic products. Canada, they concluded, could not stand the contradiction between these outside forces acting on the country as a whole and the provincial monopolies in employment.

In 1937, the Privy Council rejected most of the measures that had been passed to implement this new federal activity. A new commission, the Royal Commission on Dominion-Provincial Relations (Rowell-Sirois Commission) was then created. It seems that every new burst of federal interventionism is attended by a commission of inquiry, followed some time later by a federal-provincial conference. The organizational inner logic of these commissions will inevitably lead them to recommend an enlarged role for the decision centre that brought them into being. Quite often this is the only possible route of compromise between widely differing opinions. Using Parsons' analogy of power as the, "currency" of relations in society, one could say that it is easier to agree on the creation of power than it is to remove any from circulation.

The Rowell-Sirois Commission used the federal-provincial ceasefire and the emergency of wartime to suggest that the central government should not only take on a more important role but should actually appropriate the whole scenario. The recent discovery of the importance of fiscal policy in combatting economic cycles had a decisive influence on the commission's thinking.

It was the same scenario again at the time of postwar reconstruction and the shift toward an economy of monopolies and of mass consumption. Only an optical illusion supports the idea that the 1960s saw this trend reversed. The figures generally used to prove the existence of this turnabout are not deliberately misleading, of course, but they are not above all suspicion.

Much is made of the swing of the pendulum in the 1960s. Let it first be pointed out that the federal government had seen its debt soar by a factor of 5.5 during the years 1945–64, while the provincial debt increased by only a factor of 2.7. Whereas the U.S. federal debt rose by a mere 10 percent from 1945 to 1963, the figure was 42.5 percent for Canada. This development was thus not limited to the wartime years. It even picked up again with a vengeance in the early 1970s. As for the much-quoted figures on the rapid rise in non-federal expenditure as a share of the GNP, it must be realized that the most marked increase occurred in the area of local government expenditure. Logic tells us that where the pendulum was swinging was toward the cities.

The status of local governments in relation to the provinces is, in fact, now similar in every respect to that of provinces vis-à-vis Ottawa. The years 1960–70 saw an acceleration in their fiscal dependence. The share of federal transfers in the net income of Quebec went from 9.2 percent in 1962 to 29.2 percent in 1970, and it has since stabilized at around 25 percent. Not only is this a high percentage, but its unpredictability only aggravates provincial dependence.

Even a superficial look at innovations in social policy tells us that the initiative is usually with Ottawa, even in areas of provincial jurisdiction. There is not a single federal initiative that fails to find its way into policy at one time or another. Michel Pelletier (1974) has shown how the inspiration in this realm has always come from Ottawa, Quebec's creative input being limited in most cases to the administrative adjustment of this change. The substance of the social measures is federal: their form and their institutional framework are provincial.

In the light of the studies by M.A. and W.M. Chandler (1979), Atkinson and Chandler (1983) and Careless (1977), one wonders how anyone can still maintain the thesis of political decentralization in Canada. It is even difficult to speak of administrative deconcentration, not to mention regionalization. Here we have abandoned the realm of analysis for ideology and popular belief.

In this department we are well served. The academic and political literature — from this viewpoint, they are practically the same — are full of examples of problems that prevent the Canadian economic union from performing at its best.

- Because of the restrictions imposed by provincial securities commissions, capital, and especially venture capital, cannot move around with ease. For instance, when a small business in Grande-Anse wants to go public, it does not have access to the millions of entrepreneurs in Regina, who ask nothing better than a chance to invest in the Gaspé.
- Professional associations are preventing Toronto's surplus doctors from moving to Abitibi.
- Numerous requirements regarding language, environmental protection, and safety make it hard to standardize products nationwide.
- Provincial restrictions on transportation and communications impede the movement of goods.
- The numerous restrictions on the acquisition of production factors, especially land assemblies, act as irritants.
- The host of provincial marketing policies are harming commercialization of Canadian products.
- The preferential purchasing policies only generate additional costs.

To sum up, Canada has too many budgets, too many departments of regional expansion, too many health policies, too many highway policies, too many regulatory bodies for the same sectors, too much parallel borrowing, and too many chiefs and little chiefs. Obviously, in line with the well-known pattern, this excess of barriers applies only to "the others."

A critical glance through the literature reveals that there is not a single sector of economic activity which remains untouched by this problem. In the last few months, there has even been talk of obstacles in the Canadian cultural marketplace. Culture had been the only area to escape the dreadful affliction of these interprovincial trade barriers.

This unanimity is suspect. It is hard to understand why not a single Canadian economist, for reasons of prestige, professional curiosity or simple contrariness, has set out to prove that these barriers have played a positive role in Canada. One would be free to reject his arguments afterwards, of course, but at least a discussion would have taken place. Even in the United States, there is not the same unanimity on the supply-side or Keynesian approach. This same unanimity also tells us a lot about the audience of the Quebec economists, who have been stubbornly saying for the past 15 years that the standardization of economic policies would be dangerous for Canada.

In the next chapter, I shall try to show how Canada actually benefits from this economic balkanization; for there must be some advantages. After all, the Manitobans, Québécois, and Ontarians who profit from it are also Canadians living in this economic area. Undoubtedly, exaggerated decentralization and excessive regionalization have gratified more people than just the petty provincial potentates.

This debate on the decentralization of Canada recalls the story about the Canadian tourists in France who were amazed by its uniformity:

"Just imagine. In France, you drive 500 kilometres and the policemen dress exactly the same way. What uniformity! In Canada, they are different in every city."

"On the other hand, they can't even get coordinated on their wine and cheese. Those are different in every village."

"How right you are. At least in Canada the wine is the same everywhere."

It is all a question of priorities!

A Stillborn Tradition

Recent court rulings have dealt a number of blows, all of them fatal, to the different versions of the "pact" theory, but they have also helped nip in the bud something that was on the way to becoming a prominent feature of Canadian federalism: the federal-provincial conference. The behaviour of the federal government and the nine English-speaking provinces at the November 1981 conference had already made this institution somewhat ridiculous, of course, but this scorn had become possible and even inevitable with the Supreme Court's decision to distinguish legality from constitutionality in the federal move. By ruling that Ottawa could act on its own as long as it was prepared to accept the political cost, the Supreme Court in a sense forced the provinces to reach an understanding with Ottawa: the latter could now move alone, and opposition from the provinces would actually reduce its political costs. This is the consideration, and not necessarily any desire to find the constitutional formula most likely to hurt Quebec, that explains the English-Canadian provinces' conduct during the "Night of the Long Knives."

If they chose not to include Quebec in those last-minute negotiations, it was because they knew for a fact that Quebec's presence would rule out any agreement with Ottawa: like any other province, Quebec was demanding its compensation, probably substantial, for coming to such an understanding. Having arrived at the conviction that Ottawa could and would act on its own, they had to have a minimal understanding at any price, above all one whose very terms would make it impossible for the matter to be reopened at some future date by one or another of the parties, including the only province left out.

The immediate effect of the first court rulings was thus to change the rules of the game to the point where the mechanism of the federal-provincial conference could not operate in the same way as before. In future, these conferences could well become purely administrative meetings, having lost all capacity and so all power to make decisions. One of the last vestiges of Canada's political and federal originality has just disappeared. Unfortunately, this trend has already been confirmed by the failure of the two subsequent conferences on aboriginal rights. Not only was no agreement reached by the participants, whiich was nothing unusual in itself, but the federal government's words and actions left no doubt about its new attitude to such gatherings.

From a Quebec standpoint, the conferences of ministers and premiers have not generally been much use, and there is reason to believe that future Quebec governments will not be taking part in them with the same enthusiasm as before. Quite beyond the ill humour generated by the constitutional conference of 1981, we must expect a loss of interest, not only in the many federal-provincial committees but also in the interprovincial process.

Administrative and executive federalism usually ends in an intensification of federal-provincial tensions and Quebec-Ottawa friction, which then confirms the need for the federal government to act unilaterally or else to obtain official recognition for its infringements on areas of provincial power.

As for interprovincialism, a host of factors have contributed to turn it into a real farce: the political and ideological differences among the premiers, the absence of precise operating rules, the disparities in political power and, it might as well be stated openly, the profound contempt shown by some participants, not only toward Quebec but also toward the whole process of political negotiation. This is what makes our interprovincialism a fairly futile exercise. The very notion of provincial common fronts, preliminary consultation, common positions, and concerted action really does not make sense in Canada's new political context. Besides, we are now better able to assess the enormous gap that there has always been between the promise of interprovincialism and the reality.

Increasingly, the courts will be called upon to replace the political and administrative machinery which had been in place since 1965 and which will now have no reason to exist.

In commenting on the rise of "administrative and executive federalism," Smiley gave two reasons for the phenomenon:

a) Constitutional amendment and judicial review have been somewhat unresponsive in re-delineating the respective rules of the federal and provincial governments as circumstances change.

b) The relations between the federal and provincial wings of the political parties are not very effective in giving authoritative resolution to conflicts between centrifugal and centripetal tendencies in contemporary Canada (Smiley, 1980, p. 91).

No doubt, the first of these reasons will not continue to have the same importance. As for the second, one sees here a variation on Riker's hypothesis that the degree of centralism in the party system largely explains the degree of centralization in the federal system. As far as this goes, we can turn this hypothesis around and say that with increased political centralization, we are bound to see centralization in political parties.

Certain changes to which I have already alluded could well give the parties back a role which they had partly lost. Thus, the diminished importance of administrative federalism and the diplomatic approach in federal-provincial relations will inevitably take us back to the period when close cooperation between the two levels of political parties was the golden rule, for it was within these big political groupings that debate occurred and directions were decided on. It would be better for a provincial government to try and directly influence the federal party in office than to confront it in federal-provincial meetings.

The somewhat primitive nature of the Canadian electoral system, together with the enormous distortions it has produced, have intensified this sidelining of the parties. A provincial government can only influence the federal party in power when the latter has no members in the province or region. The inevitable reform of voting procedures, then, will give the parties a prominent role once more in the mediation of federal-provincial conflict. The weakening of the mechanism of the first ministers' conferences and interprovincial conferences will simply reinforce this development.

Finally, the fiscal crisis that is hitting all Canadian governments and the gradual disengagement of these governments from many areas of activity, could also remove an important catalyst for the existence of this federal-provincial machinery. The process of disengagement will not be painless. A new type of federal-provincial conflict may emerge over the real responsibility, to the voters at least, for the decline in government services. However, the formulae that have governed the financing of these programs give the federal government a broad immunity when voters deliver their verdict. In the long term, the need for federal-provincial coordination, sometimes political and sometimes administrative, cannot but decline.

Here we have more conflicts, but conflicts that will not impel Canadian federalism to outdo itself. For Quebec, and for Canada, here is a completely new political context.

Chapter 7

A Shrinking Quebec: *The Effect of a Biased Scenario*

It is the thing nowadays to foresee various futures for Quebec that are filled with either happiness or tragedy. One is always comforted to know that history is still prepared to make exceptions in Quebec's case and to make sure that its fate is either the best or the worst. This is an old messianic reflex which we have not been able to get rid of since the day of the Secret of Fatima.

The scenario I am outlining here has nothing to do with these grandiose imaginings. Rather, it is in the tradition of the ones we were working out in *Québec 2001: Une société refroidie* (Julien et al., 1975). The contrast with the image of Canada we have just been conveying will not be particularly striking. In both cases, we are in the realm of the colourless, odourless and tasteless. It would be surprising if it were otherwise. The two societies are so closely bound together, so comfortable in their interdependence, that they really could not pretend to be following radically different courses.

Once more, it is at its edge that the development of Quebec society is likely to be different. However, in a society of 6 million people, the edge often touches on the essence, since the force of inertia will inevitably be less powerful. Since we are discussing Quebec, nationalism is bound to come up. After all, do the two not go together?

And Quebec Nationalism?

Although they are at opposite ends of the ideological spectrum, both Dominique Clift and Pierre Vallières have recently been predicting the demise of Quebec nationalism. For Clift, it is doomed because it has been primarily an elite movement which the Québécois masses could

121

support because it held out a valid explanation for, as well as an exit from, the economic inferiority which was their lot. Today, however, nationalism has become the victim of its own success, and now that the Québécois have emerged victorious over ignorance and religious alienation and have come out of their economic ghetto, they no longer have the need for this group feeling. What interests them now is the economy and their personal destinies. From the safety of numbers, they are shifting to individual competitiveness.

For Vallières, the demise of nationalism is more a worldwide phenomenon with which the Québécois have just become associated, perhaps in spite of themselves, by the defeat of the referendum. Nationalism, like all ideologies, holds out an assurance and a code of behaviour that encourage conformity to the group. It is by belonging to the group that an individual can hope to make it. This strategy has to succeed or perish. In Quebec's case, it has not succeeded, because the strength of its opposition was underestimated. No matter how wonderful the movement may have been, we have to take note of its defeat. Moreover, in a world dominated by uncertainty where everything is in question, nationalism looks more and more like a pathological condition that has more to do with a closed mind than with openness to change.

This diagnosis provokes two kinds of preliminary comment. In the first place, this is not the first time we have listened to the obsequies of Quebec nationalism. In Quebec, the problematic process of nationalism is like that of winter itself. All it takes is for the fall to be a little too warm and some people begin to worry, others to hope. Ever since the latest last-ditch conference, hopes have waxed in those for whom nationalism is the nemesis of all civilization. Meanwhile, there was English Canada falling right into step and saying that the Québécois had finally understood that the optic of distinct nationality spelled distortion.

It was in 1959 that the theory of the demise of nationalism first made its appearance, a local variant on the rumoured demise of ideologies and a natural result of another abrupt disappearance, that of Maurice Duplessis. In those days, nationalism was frequently associated with:

- a religion, which spread all the more readily in that French-Canadian society was steeped in the worst kind of clericalism;
- a culture that was closed in on itself because of its low level of urbanization and because of the tight control held by traditional elites for whom nationalism was no negligible factor;
- highly unsatisfactory but still understandable compensation, given the lag in the province's economic development;
- a kind of intellectual backwardness brought about by an archaic system of education; and
- the tyranny of an all-powerful tradition which held that the group was the only reality, since all vision of the future was completely blocked.

Then along came the Quiet Revolution to remedy this situation: secularization would do away with religious attitudes; accelerated urbanization would oblige populations to mingle and minds to open; economic development would finally gratify the French-Canadians' aspirations to well-being; the Liberals' arrival in office would mean a complete shake-up for a political culture that was built on the worst kind of patronage; reform of the education system would finally force people to open their eyes; and new elites would dismantle tradition. In a word, every problem, real or apprehended, would be solved. Yet nationalism adjusted very nicely to this new environment. It changed from French-Canadian to Québécois and from traditional to progressive.

In 1966, there were new fears for the survival of neonationalism, which was threatened on all fronts: by the exhaustion of the Liberal party on the one hand and, on the other, by the Union Nationale's return in strength under a leader whose conversion to national thinking could easily have been taken as fairly superficial. Daniel Johnson, however, was quite comfortable with neonationalism, so much so that he made it an essential element of his electoral strategy. This same fear was felt again in October 1970, with many observers claiming that the actions of the FLQ had ruined the credentials of Quebec nationalism. It was also believed for a time that social democracy might succeed where all other systems had failed. The referendum defeat of the "yes" side was interpreted in this same sense.

This time, the danger looks more serious. The signs are certainly not lacking: the massacre of the Parti Québécois at the polls, Robert Bourassa's return in strength, the fascination with economics, the new individualistic values, the internationalism of the problems and of the young people, and the state being called into question. It is as if the Quebec Liberal party, the emphasis on personal success, and the distaste for bureaucracy are all incompatible with nationalism.

The preceding pages ought to make us consider how deeply Quebec's population has actually been affected by nationalism. If this phenomenon has mainly served the electoral purposes of the parties in power, its effects cannot have been as far-reaching as people want to believe. This being the case, its demise could not have the sombre consequences that people like to predict.

It seems probable, however, that Quebec nationalism will adjust to a new environment once again; for as long as Quebec is still a seat of power, minimal though this may be, there will continue to be confrontation between varying definitions of how it should be organized. Nationalism has no existence beyond the competitiveness that governs the relations of the different groups. All forms of nationalism enter into the strategies by which social groups try to impose their hegemonic hold on society as a whole. Consequently, they cannot appear and disappear as if by magic. In this sense, there is nothing to fear or to hope for, depending on one's point of view. There is already talk of cultural and political nationalism being transformed into an economic nationalism.

For some, this change is already pointing to the new royal road to Quebec sovereignty. Others see it as actually taking Quebec away from sovereignty. Obviously, it all depends on what type of sovereignty is involved and what vision of the achievement of sovereignty is behind this definition. Such discussion, however, surely has no place in the present study.

Ottawa and the rest of the country will certainly prefer to take their chances with this economic swing in Quebec nationalism, since it is presumed to go hand in hand with a desire to get down to the "real problems." No matter how accurate this assessment may be, one cannot help wondering to what extent the swing will benefit the Canadian population as a whole. There is always the satisfaction of having one less crisis on the horizon, of course, but apart from this negative contribution, it is difficult to imagine how the standardizing of relations between Quebec and Canada in general is going to be a step forward. Does the country really need another regional economic nationalism, whether on the old Alberta model or the new Quebec one?

Learning to do without old-style nationalism is not going to be very easy for a whole generation of Québécois, those in the 30-to-45 age group who have never known any other environment. A good number of them will not see the point of the new orientation. They will look for, and find, more attractive possibilities in purely individual solutions and in influences from abroad. Paradoxically, in this way they will come to imitate what a good number of English-Canadians have done before them, going into exile in a place such as California. For the Québécois, such places are even more plentiful and perhaps more exciting, since memories are greener of what is left behind. The departure will always be conditioned by this sense of loss. Since Quebec still offers a fair potential for development, and especially since this generation has a virtual monopoly on the skills of personal promotion, we can expect this exile to be blessed with success. It will also be without sequel, however, for Quebec and Canada.

Beyond considerations of personal strategy, there is the whole question of collective identity. Can Quebec continue to exist in another dimension than that of a mere geographical province unless it is able to project, to itself and others, the image of a distinct entity? Would a Quebec existing only in the same way as Saskatchewan or Nova Scotia still be an entity in which the sense of belonging was a trump, and a high trump, for the individuals in it?

For the real question is the profitability of Quebec's nationalism and collective identity, not just its survival. That is not in any real danger and probably never will be. It could very well turn out, however, that the new collective identity now emerging in Quebec offers nothing to those who subscribe to it. The usefulness of nationalism is what we should be talking about.

The sense of belonging does not increase the sum of our being. This is no mystical experience. It does nothing to put up dams, not even on the Manicouagan. It only adds to the quality of life through the mystery it adds to human activity. The possibility of speaking of "us" or "ourselves" is of interest only because it enriches the environment. It is a dimension that isolation or individuality cannot give. This is what makes it a collective asset as precious as pure air or efficient public transport.

For a generation, these collective "ourselves" have been increasing to the point where we can now speak of multiple belongings that intersect and crisscross, letting individual people choose among all the ways in which they are defined. The competition of these "ourselves" is the best guarantee of a fascinating life. It offers people a whole range of experiences, from the onlooker's utter passiveness to the role of the dedicated actor.

Being able to define oneself as a Canadian and a Québécois (and a Montrealer) at the same time is a value based on the tensions and contradictions inherent in these identities. But this confusion is better than simply knowing that one is a Canadian living in Ontario (and in Toronto, what is more). In such cases, all that is needed is the simple question, "Where are you from?"

There is a more immediate and determining aspect of Quebec, however, than the probable course of its collective identity. The question of numbers arises as well.

A Question of Political Demography

No federal government for the past 20 years has been willing to confront what was one of the most disturbing threats to Canada's medium-term survival as a distinct political area, namely the demographic decline of Quebec. In addition to the usual reservations about becoming involved in anything as delicate as population policy, there has been the fact that this question has a long association with the expansionist aims of Quebec governments and their obsession with enlarging their political sphere of influence and their constitutional authority. The fact that this power is shared by the two levels of government has allowed the governments of Quebec to develop a few policy mechanisms, though these have not generally yielded the anticipated results. The central government has not objected to the whole notion of Quebec involvement in immigration matters, of course, but, given this acceptance, Ottawa's sole concern has been to stop Quebec at all costs from differing from the other provinces in this regard and, most important, from using immigration as an additional window onto the international scene.

For obvious reasons, Ottawa has also not wanted to encourage movements of population from the other provinces, while it has never been a federal priority to supply Quebec with outside immigrants who could integrate with the Quebec situation. So much so, in fact, that there were practically no reservations when Quebec moved to exercise the legislative power given it in this area by the Constitution.

Quebec's demographic prospects in the federation, then, are extremely bleak. They would be just as bleak outside the federal framework, but their political interpretation would inevitably differ. At the time of the 1981 census, Québécois accounted for no more than 26.5 percent of the Canadian population. The percentage is likely to reach 24 percent by the turn of the century, taking into account the demographic variables already present.

A political party could then carry 67 percent of the seats in the rest of Canada and have an absolute majority in the House of Commons. It would be able to win an election with no representation from Quebec. Given a minimal contingent of 20 percent of Quebec's seats, all the party would need would be 59 percent of the other ridings to get the same result. As the population of Quebec declines, it will thus become progressively easier for a party to gain office and to govern without support from the voters of Quebec. However, it will reasonably be said that these predictions are really just views, and very pessimistic ones to boot, which fail to consider the country's new situation or the place held by francophones on the chessboard of power.

The linguistic make-up of the country causes still greater concern. Between 1971 and 1981, the situation grew even worse. A mere glance at the figures on language transference will convince the most hardened skeptic. From 1961 to 1971, more than 273,000 persons of French mother tongue living outside Quebec adopted English as their everyday language (Table 7-1). In 1981, when the base was obviously more limited, transfers actually increased to 304,630 (Table 7-2). For the group of French mother tongue, this meant an increase of 11 percent in losses and 4 percent in total transfers. Much has been made of this increase in the French group's gains at the expense of the population of English mother tongue (from 20,000 to 40,000), which made it possible to reduce the net balance of total transfers somewhat. The phenomenon was so restricted, however, that it was significant only in terms of percentages. In addition, as Robert Bourbeau has pointed out (1983), over 90 percent of the new acquisitions occurred in the provinces that were the preferred destinations for persons leaving Quebec. This was more a migration phenomenon, than one of language transfer. Outside Quebec, no more than 5.3 percent of citizens gave French as their mother tongue (as against 6.0 percent in 1971), a result made more surprising by the fact that record numbers of Quebec francophones emigrated to Canada during this period. When it came to the language spoken at home, only 3.8 percent of non-Québécois said they used French (as against 4.4 percent ten years previously).

TABLE 7-1 Language Transfers, Canada Minus Quebec (1971)

Transfers	Mother Tongue			
	French	English	Other	Total
Into English	273,000		1,201,700	1,475,500
Into French		20,200	5,800	26,000
Into other languages	2,600	75,500		78,100
Total transfers	276,400	95,700	1,207,500	1,579,600
Net transfers	− 250,400	1,379,800	− 1,129	

Source: John Kralt, *Languages in Canada. Schematic Studies*, Cat. No. 00–707: Ottawa, Statistics Canada, Canada Census, 1971.

TABLE 7-2 Language Transfers, Canada Minus Quebec (1981)

Transfers	Mother Tongue			
	French	English	Other	Total
Into English	304,630		1,394,520	1,699,150
Into French		40,385	5,435	45,820
Into other languages	2,795	97,585		100,380
Total transfers	307,425	137,970	1,399,955	1,845,350
Net transfers	− 261,605	1,561,180	− 1,299	

Source: Statistics Canada, *Canada Census* (Ottawa: Statistics Canada, 1981).

It is customary to use these figures to illustrate the failure of federal policies to maintain French minorities and bilingualism. This is a partisan and short-sighted reading of the situation. What should be seen in it is a most effective resistance by the country's socioeconomic reality to all attempts at linguistic rearrangement. For Quebec, this setback is more threatening than all the comfort of knowing that the figures have finally confirmed what everyone had already realized for some time, namely the English character of the rest of the country.

The scant success of language policies is not confined to the federal government. A detailed look at the results of Bill 101 tells us that Quebec's achievements in this area are really no more dazzling.

Among Québécois of French mother tongue, transfers to English rose by 45 percent between 1971 and 1981, from 73,000 to 106,000. In the allophone group, transfers to French did increase by 35 percent (from 34,000 to 46,000), but transfers to the anglophone group went up by 20 percent (from 84,000 to 101,000). The outcome, then, was discouraging to say the least. For the allophones, English still remained the pre-eminent language of attraction, 69 percent as against 71 percent in 1971. For the francophones, the net balance of language exchanges with the anglophone group remained the same, a loss of about 25,000. That such a situation can still be possible, in view of the way Bill 101 restricts access to English schools, is rather surprising. It would seem that allophones are merely following the path taken before them by the francophones and are learning English in the streets. The fact that there are no language controls on access to CEGEP and universities simply favours this trend. The assimilation occurs outside the elementary school and is only confirmed in the university.

By themselves, these figures should put paid to the hypocrisy of the statement we have been hearing since the language crisis began, namely that the allophones are only waiting a chance for unforced integration with the linguistic majority.

Canada's demolinguistic environment is characterized by two other recent developments which I must mention before attempting a general balance sheet: the phenomenon of immersion and the "Frenchification" of the federal civil service.

It is as much as one's life is worth to express a few doubts about the immersion programs. They have become like good weather. Who dares object to their proliferation? In 1982–83, there were some 97,456 children in immersion classes outside Quebec, representing 2.8 percent of total enrolment. Given this mass movement, what can one add?

What we ought to find interesting in all this is not the numbers involved but some of the arguments that accompany the love affair. All one has to do is to leaf through the immersion literature (and particularly the special issue of the review *Langue et Société* (vol. 12, winter 1984) to gauge how little things have actually changed in Canada. For example, among the numerous concerns of the immersion parents and specialists, the following are noted: the real quality of the French being learned ("Not Quebec slang! Oh my God, no!"); the quality of learning in the "true" subjects; the degree of retention; and the comparative effectiveness of the approach. Reading the articles and publications of *Canadian Parents for French*, one gets the impression that these programs are a little like pedagogical high-wire acts. French is seemingly a sort of mine field that can only be negotiated with the parents' quasi-religious fervour. Immersion is like a mysterious world from which some never return alive — psychologically, of course.

This Tupperware approach makes one smile. Yet it shows us all the artificialty of this movement. At small cost and with numerous associated advantages, including a certain snobbery, it fosters the illusion of full participation in a new Canada. Never is there any mention of the solution, so much simpler, of sending children to totally French schools where instruction and administration are all in French. They want French, all right, but only as a language and not as a culture.

There remains the issue of the Frenchification of the federal civil service. It seems that as far as "francophonization" goes, there have been satisfactory results. We must get beneath the surface a bit, but let us be good sports and admit straightaway that this is a sector where there has been genuine progress. Let us not be such good sports, however, as to forget that this is simply a question of elementary justice and that it is not so hard to find candidates when one wants to pay the price.

It is less easy, on the other hand, to create working environments where francophones can actually function in French. In this respect, the failure has been total, and this should not surprise us. Why should these francophones, accounting for 25 or even 50 percent of the working environment, make more use of French than people did in pre-1965 Quebec? At that time, they would usually make up 65 to 75 percent of the group. Forcing the Ottawa francophones to work in French would doom them to subordinate positions, confining them to a working space and promotion in which the frontiers were linguistic and not professional. It ought to sadden us that they agree to this.

This light dusting of language is creating a generation of Canadians whose bilingualism lets them neutralize and possibly even turn around the demands of Canada's new political order. The aim is not to acknowledge the special character of Quebec, still less its language equality, but rather to weaken its sole comparative advantage. It is Quebec's right to difference that they are trying to negate. No more is there a genuine Quebec society, let alone a Quebec culture, but simply a greater concentration of francophones in Quebec. Quebec has no claim to originality now except by being a vast immersion society.

Still more than all the political and constitutional finagling, this desire (for there is actual desire) to folklorize Quebec has something disgusting about it. It is founded on the good faith of thousands of parents and public servants.

There will be no disagreement that the trap of demographic determinism has to be avoided. The figures never really speak by themselves. They always need to be helped a little. In demographic and linguistic terms, all the lights are red; and we have not touched on the falling birthrate, the aging population, and the non-renewal of generations, three phenomena that affect Quebec as they do Western societies in general. For Quebec, however, these problems are not the most immediate danger. More worrying are the solutions put in place by the federal government and by other provincial governments.

Yet demographic stagnation is not the only threat to the integrity of Quebec society. We now have to turn back to the *Constitution Act, 1982* and its effects. Our subject is the dislocation of Quebec.

Dislocation

Internally, this demographic stagnation has already had devastating effects in Quebec, especially on school enrolments. The cumulative effects, however, have not yet begun to be felt. Of these, I shall mention the following:

- The very fact that Quebec's population is so dispersed geographically makes the demographic and socioeconomic balance between its regions that much more fragile. After a recovery which has been due, among other things, to the installation of regional institutions (the University of Quebec, regional health and social services centres), a permanent halt in economic growth could make this entire regional infrastructure both costly and ineffective. Since expectations have been raised, it would be unthinkable to dismantle the infrastructure.
- Quebec's hinterland, already fairly underpopulated and under-developed, could turn into a real desert without input from new elements.
- There are threats to Montreal's role as regional metropolis and cultural capital of French-Canadian and Quebec society.
- The combination of an aging populace and Quebec's loss of impor-tance demographically is bound to accentuate the conservative reflexes of a society that is being led toward a return to its minority mentality.

I have not dealt with the strictly economic consequences of this demo-graphic slowdown. All the signs are categorical, however: over the coming years, the demographic deadline will be putting Quebec's insti-tutions and its human networks through their greatest test since they were created. Now, for the first time, the dislocation of Quebec's social networks is a real possibility, which will give momentum to some of the phenomena mentioned in previous chapters: the defining of a pan-Canadian judicial-political sphere, the centralization of administration and decision making, and the loss of linguistic specificity. It is here that our biased scenario, rendered with small brushstrokes up to now, takes on its full meaning.

In the past, Quebec's institutions managed tolerably well, too well in the opinion of some, to survive certain major changes in the Quebec environment. The small number of these institutions, their common character around the church, their narrowness and paltry degree of social insertion made it possible for Quebec's social fabric to be main-tained. The shock of the Quiet Revolution was able to be mediated by the institutions and then to be reabsorbed in the considerable growth in numbers of institutions and structures.

Whereas our language, religion, and Civil Code was formerly the basis of Quebec's distinctiveness, one that was imposed more than desired, these elements have not the same importance today. It is no longer isolation that is the source of the characteristics that define Quebec society; it is the increase and interrelation of social networks: networks in social affairs, teaching, the universities, culture, the media, the unions, the bosses, the scientists. For the past 20 years, the institutional bolt has been very effectively fastened.

An unbiased assessment (if such can exist) of the autonomy, fullness, and integration-differentiation of Quebec's institutions would certainly show that Quebec compares favourably in this respect with a number of societies which have full political sovereignty. The majority of these institutions have more contacts with one another than they do with bodies that are similar but are outside the circle of Quebec's power. Here is the customary sign that there does indeed exist a Quebec system. Today, it is possible for Québécois, no matter how ambitious they may be, to have their entire careers, horizontally or vertically, within these various networks, passing from one to another as their own choices and possibilities suggest. On occasion, they decide to go outside them and work (though rarely as subordinates) in the Canadian system, because interesting possibilities arise. A number of them even have direct access to the international arena without having to go through Canadian networks.

This mobility is a tribute to the institutional empire builders of the 1960s. It also reflects the dynamism and the great adaptability of the Canadian system in that period. It really does not matter whether the adaptability was more the product of bureaucratic inertia or electoral chance: the fact remains that it existed. And that existence is made easier to verify by the fact that, for the last 15 years, flexibility has given way to rigidity and formalism. To realize just how far we have come since 1965, simply remember that today the drafting of a new preamble for the *Constitution Act, 1867*, recognizing the specificity of Quebec society, is one of the biggest obstacles to renewing the federal agreement. Twenty years ago, there was agreement on the constitution of a Quebec Caisse de dépôts (deposit fund). That was several political generations back.

Already, the Quebec networks are threatened by disintegration under budget restrictions which are largely due to the federal government's refusal to assume its proper share of their financing. Obviously, this is not the only reason. A certain organizational sclerosis, a professional corporativism and a drop in client groups are equally disturbing factors, but their destabilizing effects could have been dealt with had it not been for the federal high-handedness. Viewed from Quebec City (and the view must be appreciably the same from the other provincial capitals), there has been a very clear impression of the curious process by which federal budget decisions have been made over the past several years. First, the size of the allowable deficit is set. Afterwards, the various sector and department budgets are established. The difference between these two sums is the amount by which transfer payments to the provinces will have to be cut.

Bill S-31, the so-called reform of health services, and the trial balloons on setting national norms in the area of education all have no other purpose than to undermine the Quebec networks' integrity in the guise of better coordination and improved accessibility. Yet everyone concerned with the daily operation of these programs knows, and reiterates, that needed reforms have more chance of success if they originate at the provincial level. This is so true that the first thing the federal government usually sets in motion when it is deciding to move into an area of provincial power is the decentralization of administration.

Some Canadians have chosen to see these Quebec networks as so many parallel networks threatening the integrity of the Canadian whole. Whereas the majority of Québécois (and this time it is not entirely an elite phenomenon) view the networks as being so many loci of power, decision, and conflict, others decide to view them as a would-be Great Wall of China preventing the Québécois from giving their distinctiveness the run of the country.

In the end, our scenario is that of the dislocation of Quebec society, which could slowly turn into a society that was no longer French but simply francophone. The nuance is important.

Chapter 8

A Normative Scenario: *A United Quebec in a Distinct Canada*

It has been a relatively easy matter to provide a diagnosis — which is still, of course, open to discussion — of the political ailment being felt nowadays by Quebec and Canada, and even to go on and speculate about how these two societies may develop. It is not so easy, however, to extract prescriptions for the future from this retrospective survey. There are so many perils to avoid and so many windings to watch for that once the exercise is over, we are quite likely to be left with the same treatments that normally come up when it is time to attack the "Canadian evil": increased centralization, decentralization, working in unison, a new constitution, Quebec independence and so forth.

The patient would be on familiar ground, of course, but is this going to make him feel better? It is harder to get out of "the most serious crisis in one's history" than to deal with a quiet penchant for mediocrity.

Despite their seeming incompatibility, all these magic potions have much in common. They presume that if only the conflicts over jurisdiction, the quarrels about prerogatives, and the ideological antagonisms could disappear, Canada would feel better.

Only yesterday, the fashionable panacea was cooperation between the levels of government. Now that cooperative federalism has met a tragic end and has not really been replaced by that asymmetrical federalism which never actually got its chance, we hear of nothing but unison; not between the levels of government, but among the leading social partners. If there is one wish that the author of this study allows himself to express, it is that the Royal Commission on the Economic Union and Development Prospects for Canada can avoid lending official recognition to this new wave of clichés about the need for Canadians to agree on common objectives, to put an end to the labour problems that are undermining productivity, and to eliminate all barriers in order to march together toward the challenges that call to us. A pious hope, perhaps.

Rejecting the Extremes

I have chosen not to spend time on the extreme solutions. Given these two essentially conservative societies, though conservative for different reasons, such solutions are nothing but intellectual exercises, going nowhere, which could once again give us a false perspective. Besides, we have already accumulated an impressive series of such exercises over the past 20 years. Some commissions of inquiry have pored over them with the despair of those who know that the moment of the "last chance" has come. One still finds numerous discussions of them on the government record.

In this context, the option of sovereignty association is unacceptable to the rest of Canada. It always has been, even to those who were the best able to comprehend its profound originality and the enormous benefits it would bring Canada and Quebec. Probably it always will be, at least as a working basis, as are all the solutions with such names as special status, associated states, and commonwealth. I was not able to find a single English-Canadian intellectual or politician who could see anything in the sovereignty association formula but the worst kind of opportunism. No one ever noticed that this was another way for the Québécois to maintain a special relationship with Canada.

Should we be surprised? A society which rejects its own existence as a distinct society cannot be expected to accept solutions that officially acknowledge political equality in another society which cannot be imagined as anything but an integral part of a whole.

In Quebec's case, the "extreme" solutions — independence and sovereignty association — are actually more desirable and certainly more viable than the status quo, with the mediocrity that it generates. There is nothing very radical about this statement. Other solutions, more federal or confederal in nature, are also desirable and workable. Unfortunately, they are also unrealistic solutions in the short or medium term. Were they to be adopted, all that has happened in these last 20 years would have been nothing but mere accidents, epiphenomena. One can wish this or fear it; but it must not be counted on too much.

All these solutions are based on reasoning that was flawed from the start. They presume that Quebec and Canada will be sufficiently capable of running their own futures as to embark on a process which, as a precondition, requires that the two societies have this very ability. In this sense, the Canadian and Québécois paradoxes correspond harmoniously inside a vicious circle. The more that English Canada and Quebec slide into their own individual dependence, the more comfortable they become in a continual interdependence. As this develops, the solutions that begin with the break-up of dependence are increasingly needed, but at the same time they become more and more unrealistic, for they involve a denial of the most profound nature of these two societies.

For English Canada to come to an acceptance of solutions like sovereignty association or confederalism, it would have to be something other than English Canada, or in any case not the English Canada we now know; and if it ceased to be what it has always been, these solutions probably would be useless anyway! The same goes for Quebec. For Quebec truly to attain the status of a sovereign or confederated state (that is, to do so by means other than electoral expediency), it would necessarily have reached such a degree of independence that these solutions would already be redundant.

What we have agreed on calling the Canadian crisis has been appropriated by the main parties concerned to such an extent that it now forms an integral part of their world view and their definition of themselves.

Mediocrity is what I have to deal with here. Using the prospective jargon, I will say that there could be no question of working out in the absolute any normative scenarios describing glorious sequels. In the previous chapter, I refused to be alarmed. In this, I am not about to tell too fine a tale. My scenario project is more humble. Given the diagnosis established in the first four chapters, is it possible to turn right round in relation to what was outlined later on? At this stage in the Canadian political situation, it seems more important to me to envisage a dynamic that gets us away from the stagnation described earlier than to take the time for a detailed look at any of the numerous points where our new dynamic might ultimately carry us. This choice conditions my whole approach.

My remarks will thus be chained to the double diagnosis I made earlier: English Canada's nonexistence as a distinct society, and the threat of slow disintegration in the society of Quebec. In the pages that follow, there is no point in looking for anything but proposals related to the double dependence of these two societies. This is indeed a normative scenario, but one that has little to do with the "candy rose" that generally tinges these exercises.

The All-Important Image: Balance

"Unity in diversity," "the Canadian mosaic," "from sea to sea," "the equality of the two founding peoples," "bilingualism in a multicultural setting" . . . Canada's political checkroom is crammed with these alluring little tags, trying desperately to sum up the originality of the Canadian situation. The cycle is always having to start again, as the formulas finally prove unsatisfactory.

Although it is no easy task to define the underlying Canadian reality, we do not feel the same hesitation when it comes to determining the driving principle in the federal institutions. The pendulum image is generally accepted by all observers and participants as representing the real operating principle of Canadian federalism. The whole of Canadian political history is viewed routinely in this manner. In describing the development of judicial interpretation, we speak of phases that were centralizing or decentralizing, federative or unitary, depending on whether the court decisions were seen as favouring the central government or the provinces. Over time, a kind of official segmentation of the course of Canadian federalism has been established and left virtually unchallenged:

1867–1885:	centralizing phase corresponding to attempts to establish the central power solidly;
1885–1940	decentralizing or provincialist phase, thanks to the clairvoyance of the Privy Council judges, who recognized the centralizing tendency that was implicit in an over-literal reading of the *Constitution Act, 1867*;
1940–1960	new centralizing phase, made possible by the Depression and the war;
1960–1970	decentralizing counter-phase;
1970–	new centralizing thrust corresponding to the arrival of Prime Minister Trudeau.

There is no unanimity on the exact dating of these different phases. Never questioned, however, is the reality of the balancing principle on which the country's entire political story has hinged. This pendulum image brings with it a whole series of "ways of seeing" and "ways of doing" that have become constants in Canadian political parlance and practice:

• The extremely positive connotations of the idea of equilibrium has made the search for the ideal mid-point a continual obsession. All state initiatives and policies from both levels of government are scrutinized automatically for a balance rating. Furthermore, even if the government protagonists are not acting with this balance in mind in a given instance, what they do will still have an effect on it. Possibly, action will be needed to correct any damage to the equilibrium.

• Over the years, a genuine mythology has sprung up concerning the supposed advantages of this balance, which must eternally be readjusted. A.W. Johnson (1968), M. Lamontagne (1954), G. Veilleux (1971), and especially G. Lalande (1972, 1980) have emerged as the leading champions of the thesis which, in Quebec, has become one of the favoured theoretical arguments for dealing with separatist and excessively autonomist talk from certain quarters. For example, citizens are apparently better served and also better protected by two levels of government which are perpetually at war with one another. Whatever cannot be had from one level will be supplied by the other. A political innovation by one province is always placed on the other provinces' agendas.

- The pendulum principle automatically gives us a binary view of the protagonists. There must be two sides if there is a pendulum movement! Everything then becomes a matter of games played for nothing without prizes, because of a political arithmetic which requires both winners and losers but which also insists that they alternate to keep the game going. For there to be any game, there has to be a real possibility of losing, and since this perspective of defeat comes inevitably to dominate, the Canadian political game is most often dominated by talk of rebalancing: the "return of the pendulum," the "political weight" that must be regained, and so on. In short, this way of viewing the Canadian political chessboard steadily feeds discontent and the desire for retribution.
- Even more perniciously, this pendulum obsession has finally managed to condition not only our vision of Canadian political reality but also the criticisms and the suggestions for change that keep coming along. According to some, we must return to the balance that there was in the *Constitution Act, 1867*. Others, by contrast, say that the dice are inevitably loaded in favour of a centralizing imbalance. The dominant and, at the same time, fairly primitive quality of the pendulum image was bound to give rise to numerous appeals to get away from the federal-provincial wrangling and come to a sense of unison and a swing that will finally let the country confront the "real" problems.
- There exists, engraved on the very heart of Canadian federalism, a dynamic that ensures its balance. This dynamic is independent of all participants, who can only conform to it. Politics ceases to be the scene of power relations; it is given its own life. It is system. This is the machine run by perpetual motion.

After each event, it is now customary to tally up the score using this very Canadian arithmetic. The essential thing is to identify the winner clearly. This allows one to discover the losers, and vice versa. It also allows for formation of an *a posteriori* idea of the event in question.

In Quebec, the belief is often expressed that the so-called national policies cannot be pursued unless they are advantageous to English Canada and thus disadvantageous to Quebec. In Ottawa, every central government has always chosen to rationalize its actions by stating that in order for something to be beneficial to Canada as a whole, the measure must particularly not be for the direct and exclusive benefit of Quebec;

nor can it be associated with any binational definition of the country. In other words, it must not benefit Quebec and English Canada at the same time.

Outside Quebec, there are a number of people bent on reiterating that what is good for English Canada is necessarily good for all of Canada and thus also for Quebec.

This is odd mathematics indeed. In Quebec's case, they have come to confuse the sum with one of the parts. In Ottawa's case the sum is supposed to be completely independent of the parts. And in my last example, they acknowledge the existence of only one part, which automatically becomes the sum.

Can we envisage another political arithmetic without then falling into the trap of suggesting the abolition, pure and simple, of all arithmetic, on the grounds that it is only a distraction from new challenges to be met, challenges which presumably have nothing to do with this very Canadian way of doing things?

A Surprising Principle

Rather than thinking in terms of pendulums and of balance between parties, my scenario proposes to think in terms of equivalence and totality. Thus, we shall examine the following principle:

> What is good for English Canada is good for Quebec, what is good for Quebec is also good for English Canada, and what is good for both is necessarily good for the whole of Canada.

This statement will obviously have the air of a truism (for instance, that it is better to be rich and healthy than poor and sick). Its very simplicity makes it suspicious. After all, the complexity of the Canadian situation certainly cannot be reduced to remarks that are, of course, most disarming but are unquestionably simplistic.

This assertion must not be confused with some sort of appeal to good will. It has very little to do with the intrinsically good nature of human beings or some belief that better communications between Canadians would necessarily result in better understanding and fewer conflicts. The proximity and weight of the United States, the weak sociocultural differentiation of English Canada, the demographic collapse of the Canadian francophone element, the possible dislocation of Quebec society — with all these factors, no one in Canada is interested in seeing the other links in the Canadian chain weakened.

Turning Canada into a game played with prizes has also made it a social equivalent of the prisoner's dilemma. In this paradox, one recalls, a jailer promises each of his two prisoners a reduced sentence if he agrees to confess his crime and incriminate his accomplice. Both prisoners then decide to confess, with the result that they incriminate one another — to the great satisfaction of the jailer, who had never hoped for this much. In our case, the jailer's role is played by the United States, which takes advantage of the mutual non-confidence of the "prisoners." Both Quebec and English Canada claim to be getting out individually, thanks to solutions which are very rational in each individual case but which turn out to be harmful for all the players when each decides to act in this way.

The corollary to this statement is equally simple: to encourage all initiatives and all behaviour fulfilling these conditions, rather than letting the political tides and the cycles of party domination impose so-called balances, whose only lasting result is to bring on imbalances.

The two levels of government must stop considering themselves as the exclusive promoters of the interests which the Constitution apparently assigned to them, or which they were able to seize after some administrative or fiscal meddling. In short, Quebec must give its attention to English Canada and to the whole of Canada; English Canada must do the same for Quebec; and, above all, the federal government must stop confusing the interests of the country as a whole with measures that are equally unsatisfactory for Quebec and English Canada, on the pretext that what is bad for each of these two societies whose antagonism is dividing the country must be good for the whole.

This change of attitude must be worth as much to Saskatchewan as to Nova Scotia or Quebec. Although this should not be taken as proof that the thesis is correct — that would be too easy — it must still be said that the about-face will be as hard for Quebec as it will be for the central government or for the provincial governments of English Canada.

In Which the Parts Save the Whole

One of the most curious assertions of recent years is the one that holds that the Canadian whole is greater (or at least ought to be) than the sum of its parts. One wonders where this supplement to the collective soul could have come from. Was it the federal government's work? Why must it always be presumed that being in the centre of a problem necessarily means having a better viewpoint on it?

Compared with the United States, Canada has only one claim to originality, the existence of its two intermediate levels for the citizens to identify with: the regional level and (for want of a better word) the national level. The identification does not always occur in the same way everywhere in the country. In some cases, there is encroachment by one on the other. Thus, Quebec's national identification is stronger than the rest of Canada's. The latter as we have seen, is virtually nonexistent. This multiregional and binational character defines the parts of Canada.

It is hard to understand why the country does not choose to build on these strong points, rather than trying to bury them in the judicial and constitutional definitions of an imaginary country.

These obstacles to Canadian unity and the famous non-tariff barriers become so many strong points of Canadian specificity. In fact, who would really profit from the disappearance of the regional economic areas of Canada? Is it absolutely certain that it would be the Canadian people? How can it be imagined that they would succeed in doing as Canadians what they had had difficulty doing as Albertans or Québécois? Can one not presume, at least as a research hypothesis, that the presence of these regional and national areas within the country is actually the country's best line of defence? Acknowledging this officially might prove to be the beginning of an effective strategy for getting out of the mediocrity that threatens us. If the Québécois, Albertans, Ontarians, Manitobans . . . that is everybody, were to stick rigorously to a policy of buying at home, the only ones penalized would be the Americans and the Japanese.

If provincialism, regionalism, and nationalism (Quebec's) are blamed for all of Canada's ills, this is because the combined action of these forces is recognized as possessing a degree of effectiveness, since it has among other things, opened the way in these various territories for new social forces to emerge and function in relation to differentiated state structures.

No outside observer, especially from another era, could fail to be struck by the similarity between the Canadian situation at the century's end and that of the Italian republics of the Renaissance. Some will say, of course, that it was precisely the absence of territorial unity and a unified central government that caused their downfall. They will say this, but they are mistaken. Or rather, they forget that it was the frenzied search for this unity and for a unified government which upset the balance and allowed external forces to subjugate Italy. The Papacy and the Empire both attempted to impose their own versions of Italian unity. Numerous republics played with the idea. The Italian reality, however, always thwarted these noble intentions.

In fact, there was an Italian unity that existed well before the letter and well before Machiavelli called for it. The word Italy may have simply been an idea, but what an idea! When anyone wanted to give the concept a reality other than the one it answered to, the whole thing fell apart. Up to the seventeenth century, the Italian parts were unquestionably greater than the Italian whole, but who was complaining? Certainly not Michelangelo, and not the Medicis or Botticelli. It would be too unfair to point out that the unified nation-state of today's Italy, with its army and its national bureaucracy, lacks even the financial resources for the upkeep of the masterpieces produced in the times when Italy was divided and turned in on itself.

Let me put a stop right now to these dishonest comparisons, which do not take account of . . . .

It is surprising that in 1984 (or perhaps this is the final spasm of a symbolic date) one still dreams of central management of the Canadian economy, of strengthened coordination of the doings of the actions of the different levels of government, and of muscular unison among the social partners. The rediscovery of the regulatory efficiency of the marketplace and the new potential in the management of information apparently did not, in Canada, have its much-vaunted effect.

It cannot be denied that the different regions of the national economic area are more interested in bettering their own economic performance than in worrying about the quality of the mechanisms for nationwide coordination. The regions are using every means at their disposal to try to diversify their own economic areas and thus put a stop to their economic dependence on other regions. In the process, the provinces are erecting numerous barriers to prevent their territories from being emptied of their population and wealth. The result of this is competition among regions to attract new investment that will increase jobs. It is this disorderly race for economic development that some would like to see ended.

"To be replaced by what?" I would be tempted to ask. "By an authoritarian appropriation by the central government of these financial resources and new production capacities? If this is the case, one can wonder whether:

- this appropriation will necessarily be very different from what is currently produced by interprovincial competition;
- this appropriation will be as effective, since it will replace decisions taken at a regional level by others taken at the centre;
- this appropriation will put an end to political pressures and to the disorderliness of the process, since Ottawa's decision will inevitably depend on the relative strength of the provincial contingents in the government party;
- an exclusive appropriation by Ottawa will not be more exposed to those international pressures which are now often dispersed by two levels of obstacles;
- to this unified appropriation by Ottawa, one will not have to add regional levels in order to see to the implementation of decisions; which leaves the door open to wrangling again.

It is an ineffective kind of reasoning which assumes that the simple *pronunciamiento* of "national" norms will ensure their application. The decreeing of national standards gives a certain satisfaction, since it is a cheap way of pretending that the situation is under control and that the problem is on the way to being solved. This is a current illusion, and one that is fostered by the organizational culture of any bureaucracy.

Ordinarily, such edicts are accompanied by tougher regulatory measures which help give a better idea of the problem, which in turn renders the national code even more indispensable. Instead of working on the solution, they slave away at the problem. This is an approach encountered frequently in the universities.

Each year, for example, the faculty in many university departments note a deterioration in the quality of the students. Complaining about students and their catastrophic performance is a sport almost as popular as deploring federal-provincial competition. What makes this sport even easier is that, with time, one builds a more and more gilded image of the past. Once agreement is reached on the students' assumed inability to write under pressure, the department's decision will, irremediably, be to add an examination to the already long series of prerequisites for the diploma. The result of this is invariable: next year, a good number of students will fail the examination and complaints will only swell, supported this time by a fresh harvest of horror stories. The solution customarily used will be another, even harder examination.

Since this little game cannot last for ever, and since its consequences are too heavy for the organization, they will choose to pretend. In the long run, the examinations become tougher and tougher, while the marking gets more and more relaxed . . . and the students get less and less prepared. But the faculty will have saved face and will have had the satisfaction of knowing that the standards, even if no one comes up to them, are still identical for everyone.

The promulgation of national norms fools nobody, not even those who become their propagators. Can one think of another way to proceed?

Quebec as Well

One hesitates to list the changes that the principle stated above requires or would involve in the case of Quebec. Contrary to what some might fear — or hope — there is no question of Quebec's giving up its status as a national collectivity or as a political society. Nor is it a matter of the Quebec government, whichever it is, giving up on even the possibility of putting an end to its association with the Canadian experiment. This does not mean the right to permanent blackmail but is simply the natural consequence of Quebec's political autonomy. The one cannot exist without the other. These professions of faith and official renunciations are a bit too much like the old solemn communions at which one made a hasty renunciation, and without too much conviction, of "Satan, his pomp and his works."

The reversal of attitudes is both simpler and more difficult. For the governments of Quebec, it is a matter of practising what they have not stopped preaching since 1960, namely the equality of the two societies that make up Canada. In concrete terms, this means taking into consideration the English-Canadian reality as it was defined in Chapter 4. This may seem to be a contradiction in terms, since I defined this English-Canadian reality as one that gives relatively little room to manoeuvre, if it does not completely deny the possibility of political autonomy in Quebec. It is not so much a matter of accepting English Canada as it has chosen to define itself up to now, but of accepting it as it could be if it decided to play its real role of majority group in Canada's political, economic, and cultural space.

Many Québécois, especially among the promoters of sovereignty, will pronounce in favour of this attitude, which will readily be confused with the image of an "English Canada as English as Quebec is French," which people like to bring up as if to prove their sense of justice and openness of mind. If this were all, things would be too easy. In Quebec, we are past masters in the art of giving English Canada permission it neither needed nor cared for. Where the difficulties arise is when the time comes for Quebec to accept new politico-administrative procedures.

Mechanisms of Adjudication

We must first accept that the inevitable conflicts of interpretation and power will be decided by a court in which English Canada is present in the majority and in which the rules of interpretation are much more closely linked with Anglo-Saxon than with French judicial culture. Given the fact that reform of the Supreme Court has always been among the most insistent of the demands from Quebec governments for constitutional reform, this acceptance will be liable to arouse resistance. Nonetheless, it is a preliminary to any rebuilding of Canada on a basis which recognizes Quebec's status as a distinct political society.

When we agree to let the judicial authority rule on the evolution of the political contract in this way, we obviously agree in large measure to put our trust in the good wishes of the majority. We could always mitigate this dependence by making sure of the judges' impartiality and keeping the grey areas as few as possible, though this approach is not particularly consistent with English Canada's constitutional tradition; but when it comes right down to it, Quebec must acknowledge that its status as a distinct political society calls for recognition on its part of the demographic and geopolitical realities of the Canadian system. If Quebec wants the new Canadian contract to confirm in some degree the equality of two societies, at least to the extent that they both exist within the Canadian whole, it must also accept that the interpretation of this equality is not carried out according to egalitarian procedures.

For Quebec, the status of distinct political society will have meaning only if it is anchored solidly in a commitment to recognize that, in the long run, the agreement of the most powerful and most populous is a necessary condition. Without this *a priori* commitment, the political equality would make no sense, let alone ever have a chance of seeing the light of day. This is a prerequisite.

The End of Profitable Federalism

Given that the parties and movements calling for total sovereignty for Quebec will continue to exist, it will not be easy to get rid of the argument concerning the profitability of federalism. This is going to be as difficult as persuading a Thomist theologian to stop using his proofs of the existence of God. The profitability argument, however, should quickly stop displaying the intensity and the ledger refinements that have been so familiar for 20 years. To the extent that the political setting sheds its air of a "game without prizes," the geographical distribution of the benefits of the common political association ceases to be a life-or-death issue.

There are many cases where Quebec will have to assume additional costs which only the nationalist blackmail is fending off at present. The renegotiation of the Churchill Falls contract is one example of this. Other signs will be specialization in Quebec's agricultural sector, integration in its autonomous financial sector (caisses populaires, Caisse de dépôts), and the disappearance of some traditional monopolies (airplanes).

Sharing Certain Exclusive Areas

The realm of secondary and post-secondary education is really too important to remain sheltered very long from the exchanges between English Canada and Quebec. For the past 20 years, all the successive governments of Quebec have been fond of saying that they looked favourably on the integration of the school system of English Canada under the central government's thumb; on condition, obviously, that this integration in no way affected Quebec. But it is not that form of reorganization in the Canadian and Quebec school system that I want to deal with here. Yet again, that would be too easy.

This integration of the English-Canadian university network is already fairly advanced. The ceiling on enrolment, excess equipment, the Canadianization of programs, forced adjustment to the conditions of the job market and the standard influx of new communications technologies — all these factors did more to get an English-Canadian university network in place than all the political statements.

Up to a certain point, this movement of rationalization and integration should continue. Without a genuine system of university education, there can be no question of a distinct and autonomous English-Canadian society. However, this movement can continue only if Quebec's university system goes on developing while maintaining its sequestered air.

Unquestionably, this has been one of the preserves most jealously guarded by generations of "defenders of the sacred rights of Quebec." Yet no one will deny either that there has been a turnaround here from the spirit and letter of the *Constitution Act, 1867.* We can decide to see it as a withdrawal, therefore, or at least, *de facto* recognition of the numerous encroachments by the federal government. This recognition, in my view, is preferable to the current fiction that Quebec's university teaching is determined entirely by the Quebec authorities. The shapeless, atrophied development of Quebec's university system has been the very costly outcome of this fiction.

In concrete terms, the loss of exclusiveness in the universities could translate as:

• the elimination of some university institutions;
• the launching of a Canada-wide network of French-language universities;
• the creation of Canada-wide universities and institutions of higher learning;
• the establishment of better-integrated accessibility policies (not to mention the allotment of specializations) in order to achieve higher levels of excellence; and
• the definition of a Canadian development plan for higher learning, especially as concerns the recycling of manpower and permanent training.

There will be a strong temptation to take these recommendations out of context and use them to argue the need to impose national standards in university education. This would confirm once again how ridiculous and infantile a certain approach to Canadian problems is.

The universities form one area of activity in which it is possible for Quebec and the rest of Canada to unite some of their efforts without endangering the institutional integrity of Quebec. This sharing obviously has nothing to do with recent federal attempts to get the Quebec universities and Quebec itself into step by imposing programs that no one wanted. It is to be hoped that the Commission can tell the difference between coordination of effort and the morbid attraction of having everything standardized.

One of the main requirements of Quebec and other provinces, before agreeing to having their universities in this network, might be that Ottawa should abandon all claims to set Canada-wide standards. The objective is not to standardize the universities as if they were grain elevators, but to ensure that the most flagrant cases of duplication are avoided.

Why would Quebec agree to share in this way a resource over which it has exclusive jurisdiction? Because the advantages are significant and the political cost is minimal. In fact, it is unthinkable that the universities should be organized on any but a linguistic and geographical basis. Even with the development of new teaching technologies, the students and the courses are still the special raw materials of any university institution. One may suppose that there will never be a French university in Alberta. Except for a few institutions that are more like teaching experiments than true university establishments, all the French universities in the country, even with all the networks in the world, should be located in Quebec.

The mode of operation envisaged for this type of network exists already, in theory and in practice. Radio-Canada/CBC offers an example, in an area of federal power, of an institution that is obliged to "Quebecify" itself because of realities. Despite all the claims by certain federal politicians, Radio-Canada's market is found in Quebec. All the rest can be seen as a sort of electronic volunteer brigade, a Peace Corps of television. In a more theoretical sense, this operating mode has a name: sovereignty association. There is never anything new under the sun of political theory.

Besides, and let us admit this candidly, the primary objective of setting up the network has very little to do with Quebec, where almost no change would be called for in such a case. It is above all English Canada that would be concerned with such a measure which would have no other aim than to create, institutionally speaking, this English-Canadian entity. So long as it is not in existence, all Quebec's claims of equality will be futile.

Let us now see what this new approach requires of the federal government. The sacrifices and challenges are no less significant. Quite the contrary.

Meanwhile, in Ottawa

Seeing itself now as the big winner of the last round of constitutional negotiations, the Canadian government will have little incentive to modify its views. Why would it? The process of constitutional review is too well launched. The two most serious obstacles to the big federal manoeuvres turned out to be paper tigers: the provincial common front and Quebec. We must therefore expect the central government to pursue its centralizing approach. The laws of the electoral marketplace require it. In addition, Ottawa is the only level of government that did not reduce its bureaucratic strength during the last economic recession. The pressures favouring expansion of the federal state's role will only build. Parkinson oblige.

Thus, the following proposals will necessarily have a futuristic feel to them. It is hard to see what could trigger this turnaround in opinion. To be convinced of the sheer size of the job to be done, simply recall that barely two years ago this same government did not dare to relieve the new Canadian Constitution of its monarchical residue on the grounds that Canadians were not ready for such a break. And yet, these same conditions can be interpreted otherwise. They form a favourable environment for calmly studying the possibility of refusing to put up with the state of quiet mediocrity in which we are comfortably installed.

I have already pointed to numerous sectors in which Quebec's distinctiveness is now being threatened, most often by the levelling policies of the central government, and in which they would need to be strengthened, without this in any way prejudicing the development of Canada as a whole or, indeed, of English Canada. It is now up to Ottawa to play its part in accentuating the differences among the components of the federation. Why is it, then, that protection for the originality of Quebec society in these sectors which are deemed so crucial, has to be the exclusive and even egotistical vocation of the provincial government?

To illustrate the reversal, I am advocating (just so long as this list is not seen as exclusive or exhaustive), I shall cite five special areas for this new federal action.

- *Language*
  Encourage the gallicization of Quebec in the sectors of federal jurisdiction and thus help to extend and intensify the integrity of Quebec's social network.
- *International Presence*
  To encourage Quebec's international presence in the sectors permitted by its powers and where this international presence is particularly advantageous and difficult to secure.
- *Working in Concert*
  Encourage the setting up in Quebec of structures in which the chief economic agents coming under the responsibility of the Quebec government can work in concert.
- *Culture*
  Contribute to the mobilizing of a new impetus for Quebec's cultural development, as well as for recognition of one of the two great cultures on which the Canadian experiment was built.
- *Law*
  Accelerate the process of unifying the courts and laws of Quebec.

Two of these areas, culture and international representation, call for more explanation.

In the preceding chapter, I discussed at length one of the main dangers awaiting Quebec society and indirectly threatening all of Canada, namely the disintegration of the social networks which had slowly taken shape with help from the Quiet Revolution. To a large extent, this society is the victim of its own success. The accelerated change experienced in the years 1960–75 cannot be repeated with impunity in every generation, and fortunately so. Some recent work (Latouche 1974, Ricard 1983, Gingras and Nevitt 1983) has considerably modified what was until now the prevailing impression of this period of the Quiet Revolution, as much among the apologists as among the critics.

François Ricard implies that it was the significant demographic bulk of the famous baby-boom generation that allowed the new values, which had a marginal existence until then, to assert themselves with a vigour that one experienced. All of a sudden, one entire generation was able to take advantage of a virtual monopoly situation in jobs, education, ideologies and values. By demographic chance, this generation did not meet with any genuine competition from either the previous generation or the generation that followed. What is more, it had some relatively unoccupied fields at its disposal in politics, the arts, education, the economy and the bureaucracy. Financial possibilities, seemingly limitless, also contributed to the general excitement and the belief that everything was possible. For the space of 20 years, one was able to put into practice the two pre-eminent mottoes of the 1960s — that of Social Credit ("What is humanly desirable is financially attainable") and that of May 1968 ("Be realistic, ask for the impossible"). A curious situation.

The Social Research Group's 1959 poll, so long forgotten, confirms this new vision of the Quiet Revolution. Those events were not produced by an immense groundswell of Quebec opinion confronting a dictatorial and reactionary political regime; the Quiet Revolution was more the result of a few happy coincidences, a favourable economic situation and the action of elites, new and old, who chose to become involved in a project of national construction. Yet it really matters little what the underlying reasons were that presided at the birth of modern Quebec: the result is there. All may see it for themselves. Using demystification, however, we can fully reveal the fragility of the edifice which the revolution built.

In the rest of Canada, it is hard to imagine how this new Quebec society could really be so fragile a structure. Some congenital insecurity gets blamed for this pessimistic view of things. There can be no doubt that the sense of failure has come back strongly to Quebec's nationalist elites who have trouble accepting the results of the referendum. Nostalgia inevitably distorts their vision. But there is more than bitterness. The feeling of blockage is felt the most in Quebec's younger generations. The impression of going round and round, the conviction that everything is stymied — these are widespread feelings.

For several years, a wind of déjà-vu has been blowing on Quebec, and it shows that the passage into the 1980s was not a gentle one. The 35-to-40 generation who were in their twenties during the Quiet Revolution, are now well on their way to monopolizing all the posts of command. They have become both the producers and the consumers of the cultural and social innovations that have distinguished Quebec for the past 20 years. They do not have to pay the bill for their greatest failure, which was to have been the appearance in the political sphere of a Quebec society considered the equal of English Canada's. While getting older, they can readily make all the adjustments required by new socioeconomic conditions. They manage without too much difficulty to compensate with career challenges for the absence of competition from the younger generations.

The Sommet sur la jeunesse (youth summit) held in the summer of 1983 apparently had much to reveal concerning this sense of powerlessness. The federalism-independentism debate was left to the professionals in these fields, of course, but it was impossible to replace it with an original view of society and the place young people should occupy in it. In certain circles, the fact that young Québécois had turned down the independentist option was hailed as a significant victory. "At last the young Québécois have understood" seems to have been the cry of relief that went up in the offices of the Secretary of State. This was one of those "victories," however, which does not necessarily promise much for the future. Here, one is tempted to adapt the famous line: "If one is not independentist at 20, whatever will one be at 40?" The new passion for the economy would be described as highly promising. Nonetheless, if it were to be coupled with indifference to Quebec society, the results could be disastrous, not only for Quebec but for all of Canada; for there is no display of cultural chauvinism in affirming that without a Quebec society, conscious of what sets it apart, Canada's claim to create a presence on this continent "alongside" the United States could turn out to be baseless.

The debate in the winter of 1983 on the status of the French language in Manitoba gives a fairly good idea of what the plan for a bilingual and multicultural Canada delivers in reality. For the opponents of the rights of the Franco-Manitobans, the new rallying cry was that French was too important to belong to them exclusively. No one, neither among the federal supporters of this bilingual Manitoba nor among the Quebec critics of this bit of bilingual piecework, had foreseen this turn of events. By this refusal to afford the Franco-Manitobans the possibility of using their language and certain institutions which they would operate in their own name to create a cultural area, the idea was put in jeopardy that cultures can exist in Canada in which participating individuals find natural milieus for the enhancement of their individuality.

Contrary to all expectations, one finds in Manitoba not a rejection of French — we are past the days of protest at French on cereal boxes — but a refusal to view the language as anything but individual enrichment. For the Manitobans (and here one suspects that they are altogether representative of English-Canadians generally) the French language is a question of immersion classes and not of culture. This is no longer a problem of xenophobia but of their refusal to see themselves as anything but a collection of individuals.

These few remarks, which obviously offer nothing of sociological analysis, stress the urgency for the central government to participate in the consolidation of the cultural distinctiveness of Quebec. It is obvious this is not a role for which this government has had much preparation in recent years. For the last 15 years, the federal government seems to have been guided by one principle in this area: anything that reinforces the originality, autonomy, and difference of Quebec's culture is a potential threat to Canadian unity. Over the years, Ottawa has come to define itself in the role of promoter of a Canadian culture which, of course, does not deny the regional characteristics but which stands squarely above them. Success in this line has been fairly limited.

Up to the present, all interventions in the sectors related to culture were viewed by the main interested parties, as much in Ottawa as in Quebec City, as being directed against the cultural distinctiveness of Quebec. They were not wrong. However, one must recall that the three institutions which have contributed the most to Quebec's cultural explosion, and thus to the redeployment of Quebec nationalism, are cultural institutions of the federal government: Radio-Canada, the National Film Board, and the Canada Council. Can one think of reviving that period of state of grace?

The question of Quebec's presence on the international scene is more complicated. But is it really? Why would it not be in the interests of the whole of Canada for Quebec to secure a distinct representation on UNESCO? Would this not be an objective that is attainable, profitable and stimulating for Canadian external policy? One thing is sure: it would be an original objective and it could not be more Canadian.

Those who object to this idea will raise such questions as the unity in Canada's international presence, the erosion of the powers of the central government, the slide toward independence, balkanization, and so on. Over the years, such arguments have become so many automatic responses, their validity untested for nearly twenty years. Whereas Canada's external and defence policies undergo periodic re-examination in depth, some of their premises are never subject to the same critical eye.

One country, one external policy, one international image, one international representation, one international voice, one international signature, one international perception, one international antenna . . . . The list of the various aspects of this oneness is long indeed. But is it as simple as this equation would have us believe?

- Despite unceasing effort, this policy of oneness has partly failed, which has only weakened the federal government's international credibility and its quite legitimate claim to present its viewpoint and solutions on the big international questions.
- This desire to put Quebec in its place has monopolized a fair amount of

resources and effort which could have been better used in pursuing more profitable objectives.

- This search for oneness has produced significant distortions in the preparation and implementation of Canada's external policies. The need to promote a bilingual and bicultural image to offset Quebec pretensions has not always resulted in the happiest decisions regarding personnel and the decision-making process.
- This situation has deprived Canada of significant support on the international scene. For example, it was essentially in terms of Quebec that Canadian policy toward France was built, and this despite all the claims and attempts to free Canadian policy in France from the hypothesis of Quebec.
- Even though it has not managed to eliminate Quebec completely from the international scene, this federal purpose has been successful at exacerbating political relations inside the federation.
- In the same way, this desire on the federal government's part has forced Quebec to divert resources and energies to this sector in order to maintain its credibility and options for the future.
- The development of a ghetto and siege mentality has been promoted by all this, above all in Quebec.
- Canada's (and Quebec's) credibility on the international scene has been somewhat reduced among Canadians (and Québécois), who quite naturally tend to see the overseas initiatives of their governments as a continuation of the federal-provincial wars in other fields.

I shall not tackle here the three other sectors mentioned earlier.

A Difficult Preliminary

This scenario has very little to say about the division of legislative powers in Canada. It does not call for a complete new start for the debate on the *Canadian Charter of Rights and Freedoms*. Adjustment would be necessary here and there, of course, but that is not the main point.

The change in perspective will not occur as if by magic. Its hand will have to be forced a little. Here is where the reform of the institutions comes into play.

> This new Canadian political equation can only take shape with the availability of new levels of political relations in Canada.

This statement, too, runs counter to Canadian political common sense. Must we not, on the contrary, reduce the number of decision-making levels in Canada, rather than increasing them? Will this expansion not make it even more difficult to get unison from the political and economic agents, by increasing the locations of power and thus the potential for political battles which are as costly as they are useless? Moreover, does this not go against the trend toward "debureaucratization" and "degovernmentalization" that is so predominant in our contemporary societies? And, finally, does this not introduce a new element of complexity and confusion into relations between two levels of government that are tolerably complex and confused already?

We must institutionalize as rapidly as possible, before it is too late, if not the fact at least the principle of political equality between the political society of Quebec and that of the rest of Canada. The forms that this institutionalization can take are several: declaration of principle, constitutional preamble, confederal council. One could even innovate by thinking of an annual meeting of all Québécois members, those from Ottawa and those from Quebec City, or else a meeting of the ministers or premiers.

In fact, what I am proposing is that there should be still more politics in Canada, not less. Why should Quebec not take care (finally) of the Canadianness of the country, and why should Canada not take care of the Quebecness of its Belle Province?

Concluding in Disguise

There are two kinds of conclusions: those that recapitulate the high points of an argument and give them a further touch of brilliance, and the others, those one tries to excuse and disguise. The present conclusion clearly falls into the second group. But can a conclusion really be added to an analysis which was meant to be a conclusion itself? And conclude what? For whom? About what? Who would have thought in 1975 and 1978 that one day, discussion of Quebec would come to the point of seeking a new mode of being?

Canada, as I stated at the very beginning of these reflections, is no longer going through the most significant crisis in its history. It is no longer going through anything at all. No one seems to be complaining about this. One would think that English Canada was well pleased with the image of itself which Canada sends back. It is the hum of mediocrity.

Probably nothing will change in the next few years. The status quo is the only genuine "made in Canada" scenario. Here indeed is the drama of a country which likes to play with change and excellence but without ever letting itself go. Too dangerous.

We shall probably continue imagining the worst, a question of proving that we still exist. In the meantime, there is no hurry. Canada goes on living at a rhythm and with an agenda that others have dictated.

And what of Quebec? What of its march to sovereignty? What of the new perspectives created by the arrival of the Conservative party? What of the future of the Parti Québécois? All this will require long discussion, but that does not fall to a commission on the Canadian union. There are limits.

Nevertheless, one thing is sure. It is probable that Quebec will not readily accept the "honest walk-on part" to which it is being a little too easily consigned. English Canada, of course, would like Quebec to become an ethnic reserve, a sort of super Little Italy. The road of Canadian politics is paved with such pious hopes. /

Notes

This study is a translation of the original French-language text, which was completed in September 25, 1984.

Note in Chapter 5

1. In the matter of an act for expediting the decision of constitutional and other provincial questions, being R.S.M. 1970, c. C–180, Supreme Court of Canada, decision of September 28, 1981.

Bibliography

Alexander, David. 1983. *Atlantic Canada and Confederation*. Toronto: University of Toronto Press.

Anderson, A.B., and J.S. Frideres. 1981. *Ethnicity in Canada: The Theoretical Perspectives*. Toronto: Butterworth.

Armstrong, C. 1981. *The Politics of Federalism: Ontario's Relations with the Federal Government*. Toronto: University of Toronto Press.

Atkinson, M.M., and M.A. Chandler, eds. 1983. *The Politics of Canadian Public Policy*. Toronto: University of Toronto Press.

Banting, K., and R. Simeon, eds. 1983. *And No One Cheered: Federalism, Democracy and the Constitution Act*. Toronto: Methuen.

Barbeau, Raymond. 1961. *J'ai choisi l'indépendance*. Montreal: Les Éditions de l'Homme.

Barrette, Antonio. 1966. *Mémoires*. Montreal: Beauchemin.

Bastien, R. 1979. *La solution canadienne*. Montreal: La Presse.

Beaudoin, G. 1982. *Le partage des pouvoirs*, 2d ed. Ottawa: Les Presses de l'Université d'Ottawa.

Bell, David and Lorne Tepperman. 1979. *The Roots of Disunity*. Toronto: McClelland and Stewart.

Bercuson, D.J., ed. 1977. *Canada and the Burden of Unity*. Toronto: Macmillan.

Bernard, A. 1978. *What Does Quebec Want?* Toronto: James Lorimer.

Bernard, Jean-Paul. 1983. *Les rébellions de 1837–38*. Montreal: Boréal Express.

Black, E. 1979. *Divided Loyalties: Canadian Concepts of Federalism*. Montreal: McGill-Queen's University Press.

Boismenu, Gérard et al. 1983. *Espace régional et nation. Pour un nouveau débat sur le Québec*. Montreal: Boréal Express.

Bourbeau, Robert. 1983. "Les voies de la mobilité linguistique." *Langue et Société* 11: 14–22.

Bourgault, Pierre. 1983. *Le plaisir de la liberté*. Montreal: Nouvelle Optique.

Bourque, G., and J. Duchastel. 1983. "L'État canadien et les blocs sociaux." In *Espace régional et nation*, edited by L. Jalbert et al. Montreal: Boréal Express.

Brunelle, Dorval. 1975. *La désillusion tranquille*. Montreal: Hurtubise-HMH.

———. 1983. *L'État solide: sociologie du fédéralisme au Canada*. Montreal: Éditions Sélect.

Buck, Tim, quoted in N. Penner. 1977. *The Canadian Left. A Critical Analysis*. Scarborough: Prentice-Hall.

Burns, R.M., ed. 1971. *One Country or Two?* Montreal: McGill-Queen's University Press.

Canada, Royal Commission on Bilingualism and Biculturalism. 1967. *Report*, vol. 1. Ottawa: Queen's Printer.

Canada. 1960. *Federal-provincial Conference (Ottawa, 25–27 July 1960)*. Ottawa: Queen's Printer.

Cardinal, M., V. Lemieux, and F. Sauvageau. 1978. *Si l'Union Nationale In'était contée*. Montreal: Boréal Express.

Careless, A. 1977. *Initiative and Response: The Adaptation of Canadian Federalism to Regional Economic Development*. Montreal: McGill-Queen's University Press.

Chandler, M.A., and W.M. Chandler. 1979. *Public Policy and Provincial Politics*. Toronto: McGraw Hill-Ryerson.

Chaput, Marcel. 1961. *Pourquoi je suis séparatiste*. Montreal: Éditions du Jour.

Charbonneau, J.P., and G. Paquette. 1978. *L'option*. Montreal: Éditions de l'Homme.

Cheffins, R.I., and R.N. Tucker. 1978. *The Constitutional Process in Canada*, 2d ed. Toronto: McGraw Hill-Ryerson.

Clift, Dominique. 1981. *Le déclin du nationalisme au Québec*. Montreal: Libre Expression.

Cook, R. 1971. *The Maple Leaf Forever*. Toronto: Macmillan.

Dahlie, J., and T. Fernando, eds. 1981. *Ethnicity, Power and Politics in Canada*. Toronto: Methuen.

Daignault, Richard. 1981. *Lesage*. Montreal: Libre Expression.

D'Allemagne, André. 1974. *Le RIN et les débuts du mouvement Indépendantiste québécois*. Montreal: Éditions l'Étincelle.

Dion, Léon. 1975. *Nationalisme et politique au Quebec*. Montreal: Hurtubise-HMH.

———. 1980. *Le Québec et le Canada : les voies de l'avenir*. Montreal: Québecor.

Durham, Earl of. 1969 ed. of 1839. *Report on the Affairs of British America*. Montreal: Editions Sainte-Marie. Original English quotations taken from Charles Lucas ed., vol. 2: Oxford, 1912.

Elkin, Frederick. 1973. *Rebels and Colleagues: Advertising and Social Change in French Canada*. Montreal: McGill-Queen's University Press.

Elliott, J.L., ed. 1979. *Two Nations, Many Cultures*. Scarborough: Prentice-Hall.

Forbes, E.R. 1979. *Maritime Rights: The Maritime Rights Movement, 1879–1927*. Montreal: McGill-Queen's University Press.

Gingras, François-Pierre, and Neil Nevitt. 1983. "La révolution en plan et le paradigme en cause." *Canadian Journal of Political Science* 16 (4): 691–716.

Godin, Pierre. 1980. *Daniel Johnson : La passion au pouvoir, 1946–64*. Montreal: Éditions de l'Homme.

Goldstein, J.E., and R.M. Bienvenue, eds. 1980. *Ethnicity and Ethnic Relations in Canada*. Toronto: Butterworth.

Granatstein, J.L., and P. Stevens, eds. 1972. *Forum: Canadian Life and Letters 1920–70*. Toronto: University of Toronto Press.

Grant, G. 1965. *Lament for a Nation: The Defeat of Canadian Nationalism*. Toronto: Carleton University Library.

Gros D'Aillon, Paul. 1979. *Daniel Johnson : L'égalité avant l'indépendance*. Montreal: Stanke.

Groupe de recherches sociales (GRS). 1980. *Les élécteurs québécois en 1960*. Montreal: GRS.

———. 1962. *Les préférences politiques des électeurs québécois en 1962*. Montreal: GRS.

Hamelin, Jean, and André Gagnon. 1969. "La vie politique au Québec de 1958 à 1966." In *Quatre élections provinciales au Québec: 1956–66*, edited by Vincent Lemieux. Quebec City: Les Presses de l'Université Laval.

Heintzman, Ralph. 1983. "The Political Culture of Québec, 1840–1960." *Canadian Journal of Political Science* 16 (1): 3–60.

Holmes J. 1966. "Nationalism in Canadian Foreign Policy." In *Nationalism in Canada*, edited by P. Russell. Toronto: McGraw-Hill.

Horowitz, Gad. 1965. "Canada." *Canadian Forum* 2 (5): 93–109.

———. 1966. "Conservatism, Liberalism and Socialism in Canada: An Interpretation." *Canadian Journal of Political Science* 32 (2).

———. 1978. "Notes on Conservatism, Liberalism and Socialism." *Canadian Journal of Political Science* 11 (2): 383–389.

In collaboration. 1980. *Un pays incertain. Réflexions sur le Québec post-référendaire*. Montreal: Québec-Amérique.

Jobin, Carol. 1978. *Les enjeux économiques de la nationalisation de l'électricité*. Montreal: Albert St.-Martin.

Johnson, A.W. 1968. "The Dynamics of Federalism in Canada." *Canadian Journal of Political Science* 1 (1): 18–39.

Johnson, Daniel. 1965. *Égalité ou indépendance*. Montreal: Éditions de l'Homme.

Julien, P.A., P. Lamonde, and D. Latouche. 1975. *Québec 2001 : Une société refroidie*. Montreal: Boréal Express.

LaLande, Gilles. 1972. *Pourquoi le fédéralisme : Contribution d'un Québécois à l'intelligence du fédéralisme*. Montreal: HMH-Hurtubise.

———, 1980. "Le système politique québécoise et la dynamique fédérale." In *Le système politique québécois*, edited by D. Latouche and E. Cloutier. Montreal: Hurtubise-HMH.

Lamontagne, M. 1954. *Le fédéralisme canadien*. Quebec City: Les Presses de l'Université Laval.

Larochelle, Louis. 1982. *En flagrant délit du pouvoir*. Montreal: Boréal Express.

LaTerreur, Marc. 1973. *Les tribulations des conservateurs au Québec*. Montreal: Les Presses de l'Université Laval.

Latouche, Daniel. 1974. "La vraie nature de la Révolution tranquille." *Canadian Journal of Political Science* 7 (4): 525–536.

Laurence, Gérard. 1982. "Le début des affaires publiques à la télévision québécoise 1952–1957." *Revue d'histoire de l'Amérique française* 38 (2): 213–241.

Laurendeau, André. 1970. *Ces choses qui nous arrivent*. Montreal: Hurtubise-HMH.

Laxer, James. 1974. *Canada's Energy Crisis*. Toronto: James Lorimer.

Layson, Walter. 1981. "Who is Sovereign in Canada". Palo Alto: Stanford University. Mimeographed.

Lemieux, Vincent. 1969. "Les plate-formes électorales des partis." In *Quatre élections provinciales au Québec: 1956–1966*, edited by Vincent Lemieux. Quebec City: Les Presses de l'Université Laval.

Lemieux, Vincent, and Raymond Hudon. 1975. *Patronage et politique au Québec, 1944–1972*. Montreal: Boréal Express.

Lesage, Jean. 1962. "Marks by the Honourable Jean Lesage", interprovincial conference, Victoria, August 7, 1962.

Lescop, Renée. 1981. *Le parti québécois du Général de Gaulle*. Montreal: Boréal Express.

Levitt, K. 1970. *Silent Surrender*. Toronto: Macmillan.

Lipset, S.M. 1970. *Revolution and Counter-Revolution*. 2d ed. New York: Doubleday.

Lower, Arthur. 1964. *Colony to Nation*. 4th ed. Don Mills: Longmans.

Mathews, Ralph. 1983. *The Creation of Regional Dependency*. Toronto: University of Toronto Press.

McCallum, John. 1980. *Unequal Beginnings. Agriculture and Economic Development in Québec and Ontario until 1870*. Toronto: University of Toronto Press.

McWhinney, Edward. 1979. *Québec and the Constitution, 1960–1978*. Toronto: University of Toronto Press.

———. 1982. *Canada and the Constitution, 1979–1982*. Toronto: University of Toronto Press.

Meekison, J. Peter, ed. 1976. *Canadian Federalism: Myth or Reality?* 3d ed. Toronto: Methuen.

Meisel, John. 1978. "J'ai le goût du Québec but I like Canada." In *Le Canada face à son destin*, edited by R. Simeon. Quebec City: Les Presses de l'Université Laval.

Monière, Denis. 1979. *Les enjeux du référendum*. Montreal: Editions Québec-Amérique.

———. 1983. *André Laurendeau*. Montreal: Éditions Québec-Amérique.

Morton, W.L. 1972. *The Canadian Identity*, 2d ed. Toronto: University of Toronto Press.

Office de planification et de développement du Québec (OPDQ). 1979. *Politiques fédérales et économie du Québec*, 2d ed. Québec City: OPDQ.

O'Neill, Pierre, and Jacques Benjamin. 1978. *Les mandarins du pouvoir*. Montreal: Québec-Amérique.

Orban, E. et al. 1981. *Mécanismes pour une nouvelle Constitution*. Ottawa: Les Presses de l'Université d'Ottawa.

Patry, A. 1980. *Le Québe dans le monde*. Montreal: Leméac.

Paul, Victor, ed. 1982. *The Canadian Constitutions & Les Constitutions canadiennes, 1763–1982*. Victoriaville: Les Publications Vic.

Philips, Paul. 1982. *Regional Disparities*. Toronto: James Lorimer.

Pinard, Maurice. 1969. "La rationalité de l'électorat: le cas de 1962." In *Quatre élections provinciales au Québec: 1956–1966*, edited by Vincent Lemieux. Quebec City: Les Presses de l'Université Laval.

Provencher, Jean. 1973. *René Lévesque, portrait d'un Québécois*. Montreal: Éditions La Presse.

Québec. Commission constitutionnelle du Parti libéral du Québec. 1980. *Une nouvelle fédération canadienne*. Montreal: Parti libéral du Québec.

Québec. Gouvernement du Québec. 1979. *La nouvelle entente Québec-Canada*. Québec: Conseil exécutif.

Quinn, Herbert F. 1974. *The Union Nationale: Québec Nationalism from Duplessis to Lévesque*, 2d ed. Toronto: University of Toronto Press.

Remillard, Gil. 1980. *Le fédéralisme canadien*. Montreal: Éditions Québec-Amérique.

Resnick, Philip. 1977. *The Land of Cain. Class and Nationalism in English Canada 1945–1975*. Vancouver: New Star Books.

Ricard, F. 1983. "Tableau d'une génération en forme de déferlement." *Liberté* 150: 76–87.

Rocher, François. 1982. "Essai pour une problématique d'interprétation des conflits entre paliers gouvernementaux au Canada depuis 1960. Research notes. Montreal: Université de Montréal.

Roy, Jean-Louis. 1971. *Les programmes électoraux du Québec: 1931–1966*. Montreal: Leméac.

———. 1976. *La marche des Québécois. Le temps des ruptures (1945–1960)*. Montreal: Leméac.

———. 1978. *Le choix d'un pays*. Montreal: Leméac.

Russell, P., ed. 1966. *Nationalism in Canada*. Toronto: McGraw-Hill.

Simeon, Richard. 1973. *Federal-Provincial Diplomacy: The Making of Recent Policy in Canada*. Toronto: University of Toronto Press.

———. 1978. Introduction to *Le Canada face à son destin*, edited by Richard Simeon. Quebec City: Les Presses de l'Université Laval.

———. ed. 1979. *Intergovernmental Relations and the Challenge to Canadian Federalism*. Kingston: Queen's University, Institute of Intergovernmental Relations.

———. 1980. *A Citizen's Guide to the Constitutional Question*. Toronto: Gage.

Smiley, D.V. 1967. *The Canadian Political Nationality*. Toronto: Methuen.

———. 1976. *Canada in Question: Federalism in the Eighties*. 2d ed. Toronto: McGraw-Hill.

———. 1980. *Canada in Question: Federalism in the Eighties*. 3d ed. Toronto: McGraw-Hill.

Stevenson, Garth. 1979. *Unfulfilled Union*. Toronto: Macmillan.

———, 1981. "The Political Economy Tradition and Canadian Federalism." *Studies in Political Economy* 5: 113–34.

Stevenson, G., and L. Pratt, eds. 1981. *Western Separatism: The Myths, Realities and Dangers*. Edmonton: Hurtig.

Taylor, R.T. 1975. *The History of Canadian Business*. Toronto: McClelland and Stewart.

Trudeau, P.E. 1956. *La grève de l'amiante*. Montreal: Éditions Cité-Libre.

———. 1967. *Le fédéralisme et la société canadienne-française*. Montreal: Hurtubise-HMH. Published in translation as *Federalism and the French-Canadians*.

Vallières, P. 1982. "Vers un Québec post-nationaliste, idéologies et valeurs: oppositions, contradictions et impasses." In *Changer de société*, edited by S. Proulx and P. Vallières. Montreal: Québec-Amérique.

Veilleux, G. 1971. *Les relations intergouvernementales au Canada, 1867–1967*. Montreal: Les Presses de l'Université du Québec.

White, W.L. et al. 1979. *Canadian Confederation: A Decision-Making Analysis*. Toronto: Macmillan.

THE COLLECTED RESEARCH STUDIES

Royal Commission on the Economic Union and Development Prospects for Canada

ECONOMICS

Income Distribution and Economic Security in Canada (Vol.1), *François Vaillancourt, Research Coordinator*

Vol. 1   Income Distribution and Economic Security in Canada, *F. Vaillancourt* (C)*

Industrial Structure (Vols. 2-8), *Donald G. McFetridge, Research Coordinator*

Vol. 2   Canadian Industry in Transition, *D.G. McFetridge* (C)
Vol. 3   Technological Change in Canadian Industry, *D.G. McFetridge* (C)
Vol. 4   Canadian Industrial Policy in Action, *D.G. McFetridge* (C)
Vol. 5   Economics of Industrial Policy and Strategy, *D.G. McFetridge* (C)
Vol. 6   The Role of Scale in Canada–US Productivity Differences, *J.R. Baldwin and P.K. Gorecki* (M)
Vol. 7   Competition Policy and Vertical Exchange, *F. Mathewson and R. Winter* (M)
Vol. 8   The Political Economy of Economic Adjustment, *M. Trebilcock* (M)

International Trade (Vols. 9-14), *John Whalley, Research Coordinator*

Vol. 9   Canadian Trade Policies and the World Economy, *J. Whalley with C. Hamilton and R. Hill* (M)
Vol. 10 Canada and the Multilateral Trading System, *J. Whalley* (M)
Vol. 11 Canada–United States Free Trade, *J. Whalley* (C)
Vol. 12 Domestic Policies and the International Economic Environment, *J. Whalley* (C)
Vol. 13 Trade, Industrial Policy and International Competition, *R. Harris* (M)
Vol. 14 Canada's Resource Industries and Water Export Policy, *J. Whalley* (C)

Labour Markets and Labour Relations (Vols. 15-18), *Craig Riddell, Research Coordinator*

Vol. 15 Labour-Management Cooperation in Canada, *C. Riddell* (C)
Vol. 16 Canadian Labour Relations, *C. Riddell* (C)
Vol. 17 Work and Pay: The Canadian Labour Market, *C. Riddell* (C)
Vol. 18 Adapting to Change: Labour Market Adjustment in Canada, *C. Riddell* (C)

Macroeconomics (Vols. 19-25), *John Sargent, Research Coordinator*

Vol. 19 Macroeconomic Performance and Policy Issues: Overviews, *J. Sargent* (M)
Vol. 20 Post-War Macroeconomic Developments, *J. Sargent* (C)
Vol. 21 Fiscal and Monetary Policy, *J. Sargent* (C)
Vol. 22 Economic Growth: Prospects and Determinants, *J. Sargent* (C)
Vol. 23 Long-Term Economic Prospects for Canada: A Symposium, *J. Sargent* (C)
Vol. 24 Foreign Macroeconomic Experience: A Symposium, *J. Sargent* (C)
Vol. 25 Dealing with Inflation and Unemployment in Canada, *C. Riddell* (M)

Economic Ideas and Social Issues (Vols. 26 and 27), *David Laidler, Research Coordinator*

Vol. 26 Approaches to Economic Well-Being, *D. Laidler* (C)
Vol. 27 Responses to Economic Change, *D. Laidler* (C)

* (C) denotes a Collection of studies by various authors coordinated by the person named.
  (M) denotes a Monograph.

POLITICS AND INSTITUTIONS OF GOVERNMENT

Canada and the International Political Economy (Vols. 28-30), *Denis Stairs and Gilbert R. Winham, Research Coordinators*

Vol. 28 Canada and the International Political/Economic Environment, *D. Stairs and G.R. Winham* (C)
Vol. 29 The Politics of Canada's Economic Relationship with the United States, *D. Stairs and G.R. Winham* (C)
Vol. 30 Selected Problems in Formulating Foreign Economic Policy, *D. Stairs and G.R. Winham* (C)

State and Society in the Modern Era (Vols. 31 and 32), *Keith Banting, Research Coordinator*

Vol. 31 State and Society: Canada in Comparative Perspective, *K. Banting* (C)
Vol. 32 The State and Economic Interests, *K. Banting* (C)

Constitutionalism, Citizenship and Society (Vols. 33-35), *Alan Cairns and Cynthia Williams, Research Coordinators*

Vol. 33 Constitutionalism, Citizenship and Society in Canada, *A. Cairns and C. Williams* (C)
Vol. 34 The Politics of Gender, Ethnicity and Language in Canada, *A. Cairns and C. Williams* (C)
Vol. 35 Public Opinion and Public Policy in Canada, *R. Johnston* (M)

Representative Institutions (Vols. 36-39), *Peter Aucoin, Research Coordinator*

Vol. 36 Party Government and Regional Representation in Canada, *P. Aucoin* (C)
Vol. 37 Regional Responsiveness and the National Administrative State, *P. Aucoin* (C)
Vol. 38 Institutional Reforms for Representative Government, *P. Aucoin* (C)
Vol. 39 Intrastate Federalism in Canada, *D.V. Smiley and R.L. Watts* (M)

The Politics of Economic Policy (Vols. 40-43), *G. Bruce Doern, Research Coordinator*

Vol. 40 The Politics of Economic Policy, *G.B. Doern* (C)
Vol. 41 Federal and Provincial Budgeting, *A.M. Maslove, M.J. Prince and G.B. Doern* (M)
Vol. 42 Economic Regulation and the Federal System, *R. Schultz and A. Alexandroff* (M)
Vol. 43 Bureaucracy in Canada: Control and Reform, *S.L. Sutherland and G.B. Doern* (M)

Industrial Policy (Vols. 44 and 45), *André Blais, Research Coordinator*

Vol. 44 Industrial Policy, *A. Blais* (C)
Vol. 45 The Political Sociology of Industrial Policy, *A. Blais* (M)

LAW AND CONSTITUTIONAL ISSUES

Law, Society and the Economy (Vols. 46-51), *Ivan Bernier and Andrée Lajoie, Research Coordinators*

Vol. 46 Law, Society and the Economy, *I. Bernier and A. Lajoie* (C)
Vol. 47 The Supreme Court of Canada as an Instrument of Political Change, *I. Bernier and A. Lajoie* (C)
Vol. 48 Regulations, Crown Corporations and Administrative Tribunals, *I. Bernier and A. Lajoie* (C)
Vol. 49 Family Law and Social Welfare Legislation in Canada, *I. Bernier and A. Lajoie* (C)
Vol. 50 Consumer Protection, Environmental Law and Corporate Power, *I. Bernier and A. Lajoie* (C)
Vol. 51 Labour Law and Urban Law in Canada, *I. Bernier and A. Lajoie* (C)

COMMISSION ORGANIZATION

Chairman
Donald S. Macdonald

Commissioners

Clarence L. Barber	William M. Hamilton	Daryl K. Seaman
Albert Breton	John R. Messer	Thomas K. Shoyama
M. Angela Cantwell Peters	Laurent Picard	Jean Casselman-Wadds
E. Gérard Docquier	Michel Robert	Catherine T. Wallace

Senior Officers

Executive Director
J. Gerald Godsoe

Director of Policy Alan Nymark	*Senior Advisors* David Ablett Victor Clarke	*Directors of Research* Ivan Bernier Alan Cairns
Secretary Michel Rochon	Carl Goldenberg Harry Stewart	David C. Smith
Director of Administration Sheila-Marie Cook	*Director of Publishing* Ed Matheson	*Co-Directors of Research* Kenneth Norrie John Sargent

Research Program Organization

Economics	Politics and the Institutions of Government	Law and Constitutional Issues
Research Director David C. Smith	*Research Director* Alan Cairns	*Research Director* Ivan Bernier
Executive Assistant & Assistant Director (Research Services) I. Lilla Connidis	*Executive Assistant* Karen Jackson	*Executive Assistant & Research Program Administrator* Jacques J.M. Shore
Coordinators David Laidler Donald G. McFetridge Kenneth Norrie* Craig Riddell John Sargent* François Vaillancourt John Whalley	*Coordinators* Peter Aucoin Keith Banting André Blais Bruce Doern Richard Simeon Denis Stairs Cynthia Williams Gilbert R. Winham	*Coordinators* Clare F. Beckton Ronald C.C. Cuming Mark Krasnick Andrée Lajoie A. Wayne MacKay John J. Quinn
Research Analysts Caroline Digby Mireille Ethier Judith Gold Douglas S. Green Colleen Hamilton Roderick Hill Joyce Martin	*Research Analysts* Claude Desranleau Ian Robinson *Office Administration* Donna Stebbing	*Administrative and Research Assistant* Nicolas Roy *Research Analyst* Nola Silzer

*Kenneth Norrie and John Sargent co-directed the final phase of Economics Research with David Smith